WOODROW WILSON CENTER SERIES

RESHAPING RUSSIAN ARCHITECTURE

Reshaping
Russian architecture

Western technology, utopian dreams

Edited by
WILLIAM C. BRUMFIELD

WOODROW WILSON INTERNATIONAL
CENTER FOR SCHOLARS

AND

CAMBRIDGE UNIVERSITY PRESS
Cambridge
New York   Port Chester   Melbourne   Sydney

Published by the Press Syndicate of the University of Cambridge
The Pitt Building, Trumpington Street, Cambridge CB2 1RP
40 West 20th Street, New York, NY 10011, USA
10 Stamford Road, Oakleigh, Melbourne 3166, Australia

© Woodrow Wilson International Center for Scholars 1990

First published 1990

Printed in the United States of America

Library of Congress Cataloging-in-Publication Data
Reshaping Russian architecture: Western technology, utopian dreams /
edited by William C. Brumfield.
    p.   cm. – (Woodrow Wilson Center series)
ISBN 0-521-39418-X
1. Architecture – Russian S.F.S.R. 2. Architecture, Modern – 19th
century – Russian S.F.S.R. 3. Architecture, Modern – 20th century –
Russian S.F.S.R. 4. Neoclassicism (Architecture) – Russian S.F.S.R.
5. Constructivism (Architecture) – Russian S.F.S.R. I. Brumfield,
William Craft, 1944–   . II. Series.
NA1187.R47   1990
720′.947′0904–dc20

        90-1433
        CIP

British Library Cataloguing in Publication Data
Reshaping Russian architecture: Western technology, utopian
dreams. – (Woodrow Wilson Center series).
1. Russia. Architecture, history
I. Brumfield, William C. II. Series
720.947

ISBN 0-521-39418-X hardback

WOODROW WILSON INTERNATIONAL CENTER FOR SCHOLARS

The Center is the "living memorial" of the United States of America to the nation's twenty-eighth president, Woodrow Wilson. The U.S. Congress established the Woodrow Wilson Center in 1968 as an international institute for advanced study, "symbolizing and strengthening the fruitful relationship between the world of learning and the world of public affairs." The Center opened in 1970 under its own presidentially appointed board of directors.

In all its activities, the Woodrow Wilson Center is a nonprofit, non-partisan organization, supported financially by annual appropriations from the U.S. Congress and contributions from foundations, corporations, and individuals. Conclusions or opinions expressed in Center publications are those of the authors and do not necessarily reflect the views of the Center staff, fellows, trustees, advisory groups, or any individuals or organizations that provide financial support to the Center.

Woodrow Wilson International Center for Scholars
Smithsonian Institution Building
1000 Jefferson Drive, S.W.
Washington, D.C. 20560
(202) 357-2429

CONTENTS

ILLUSTRATIONS

xiv

ACKNOWLEDGMENTS

This volume has its origins in a series of presentations on modern Russian architecture sponsored by the Kennan Institute for Advanced Russian Studies in 1987 and 1988. Although the initial papers and discussions of the four contributors have since been substantially expanded and revised, the shared interests that ensued from these meetings stimulated us to think of producing a book that would deal with certain of the forces reshaping Russian (and Soviet) architecture in this century. Having achieved our goal, we would like to express appreciation to Peter Reddaway, who was secretary of the Institute when three of the papers were originally presented, and who supported their publication in 1988 as a Kennan Institute Special Report (*Architecture and the New Urban Environment: Western Influences on Modernism in Russia and the USSR*). Emily Pyle, formerly editor at the Kennan Institute, prepared the manuscript of this report for publication.

During the process of compiling the present volume, a number of colleagues offered advice and helpful criticism. I am grateful for the encouragement and support of Charles Blitzer, director of the Woodrow Wilson International Center for Scholars, and of Blair Ruble, director of the Kennan Institute. At the Center's Publications Program, Shaun Murphy and Glenn LaFantasie, current director, assisted in many indispensable ways. Beatrice Rehl, fine arts editor at Cambridge University Press, skillfully guided the manuscript through the process of reading and editorial review. The task of entering revisions in the drafts of the manuscript was facilitated by Lori Hylton, research intern at the Kennan Institute; and Jane Hedges edited the final manuscript with admirable precision. I am also indebted to the College of Arts and Sciences at Tulane University for facilitating my work in Russian architectural history. The Office of Printing and Photo-

ACKNOWLEDGMENTS graphic Services at the Smithsonian Institution and the Photographic Archives of the National Gallery of Art maintained their usual high standards in printing the photographs for this book. The generous cooperation of so many people and institutions has made the complex business of assembling this book both pleasant and stimulating.

WCB

EDITOR'S NOTE

In transliterating Russian terms and names into English, this volume adheres to the Library of Congress system. Rare exceptions have been made in the case of names (such as that of the writer Ilya Ehrenburg) that have become widely known under a different spelling system. Every attempt has been made to standardize documentary references in the chapters of the four authors, but this does not exclude the possibility of an occasional idiosyncratic usage in note style.

INTRODUCTION

William C. Brumfield

T HE development of Russian architecture has involved
Western concepts, and architects imported from the
West, since at least the fifteenth century, when a series
of Italian architect-engineers began rebuilding the Moscow
Kremlin during the reign of Ivan the Great. Indeed, architecture was the first of the arts in Russia to experience Western
influence in specific, documented, and usually highly idiosyncratic terms. With the founding of St. Petersburg in 1703,
Peter the Great initiated a new era in Russian architecture,
one irrevocably turned toward the West, even though it maintained a distinctive identity characterized by the unparalleled
scale of construction and the continuing presence of traditional elements in Russian Orthodox Church design.

For the next century, the adaptation of Western architectural forms to the Russian environment proceeded under
the guidance of a centralized state, whose rulers applied
apparently limitless resources to grandiose monuments and
sweeping plans for urban development. The varieties of neoclassicism supplanted those of the baroque, but the unchang-
ing constant was a belief in the ability of a supreme autocratic
power to reshape the physical environment—indeed, the very
identity of the nation itself. The discrepancy between this
ideal of rational design (embodied in the evolving plan of St.
Petersburg) and the reality of both Russian existence and the
forces of nature has been the subject of some of the greatest
works in Russian literature, most notably Alexander Pushkin's epic poem "The Bronze Horseman" (1831), whose nar-
rative of destruction and the loss of reason within an ordered
environment begins with a paean to the glories of St. Petersburg's imperial architecture.

By the 1840s the imperial design in Russian architecture
had lost its sustaining confidence and power, for reasons that
involved not only a fundamental social transformation within

I

Russia but also changes in aesthetic values and technical capabilities in European architecture generally. The details of this evolution, which created various forms of eclecticism and historicism in Russian architecture, are beyond the scope of the present study; however, the process of technological innovation and the increased role of civil engineering in architectural design led to a new stage of interaction with the West, even as Russian architects debated the possibility of creating a distinctively national architecture.

Whatever the results of the debate over style ("rational" versus "national") in Russian architectural journals during the last three decades of the nineteenth century, the imperial court and the nobility had yielded to the entrepreneurs of Russia's nascent capitalist economy as the dominant force in urban construction. In consequence, a relatively coherent style such as neoclassicism was replaced by an architecture in service to private capital and the individual owner, and the notion of a comprehensive system for incorporating ideas from the West quickly vanished. As city development proceeded in a haphazard way, often frustrated by individual property rights, emphasis shifted toward the technological tasks of building large investment projects such as banks, office buildings, department stores, apartment houses, hotels—usually funded by insurance companies and groups of stockholders.

In this context architectural style assumed a decorative function determined by the architect and his clients and often linked to an ideological program, such as the nationalism of the "pseudo-Russian" style (compare Shervud's design for the Historical Museum or Aleksandr Pomerantsev's design for the exterior of the Upper Trading Rows—both on Red Square). Western innovations in technology and materials (iron structural components, plate glass, and reinforced concrete, which appeared in Russia on a noticeable scale in the 1890s) existed behind facades that often suggested little about the tectonic system of the structure.

At the beginning of the twentieth century, the urgency of the debate over a national style faded, as economic pragmatism asserted its need for functional buildings in service to commerce. Frequent reports in the Russian architectural press on the growth of American cities and the creation of a new idiom in American architecture (particularly the skyscraper) did not, however, lead to the practical assimilation of American building methods such as the skeletal steel frame. The Russian economy and its industrial base could not pro-

2

duce the materials or the demand to justify a technologically intensive system of construction. To be sure, forms of European modernism such as art nouveau and *Jugendstil* had a significant impact on the new architecture of Petersburg, Moscow, and other major cities; yet even this style moderne had numerous, well-placed opponents in the press and yielded after a few years of creative vigor to an amalgam of functional structures cloaked in retrospective decorative motifs.

The revival of neoclassicism in Russia during the decade before the First World War parallels developments elsewhere in European architecture; but the ideological reaction against early modernism in Russia included an attack—from both the left and the monarchist right—against the basic values of the capitalist economic system that underlay urban construction. The harsh criticism of excessive "individualism" in creativity, the condemnation of the "chaos" of styles in buildings constructed for speculative purposes, the call for a return to a unified aesthetics of architectural design (derived from neoclassicism)—all implied a rejection of a culture based on bourgeois, entrepreneurial values. A particularly explicit statement of this rejection came from the influential critic Georgii Lukomskii, who wrote in the cultural journal *Apollon* in 1913 (no. 2) that great architecture derives from the power of the state and church: "For just this reason, the entire epoch of bourgeois and democratic modernism has given Petersburg *nothing*. Only the restoration of previous architectural canons can increase the beauty of our city."

Consequently, even during Russia's brief experiment in capitalist development, the ideal of a comprehensive, monistic approach to urban planning and architectural design that had flourished under imperial autocrats reappeared as a response to the general crisis of confidence in the prerevolutionary social order. In this respect architecture—and architectural criticism—played a significant role in the heated debates over the direction of Russian culture and prepared the way for the idealistic, utopian concepts of design following the 1917 revolution.

Paradoxically, the first postrevolutionary decade assimilated both the creative individualism of modernist architecture and the dreams of a regulated environment, facilitated by state ownership of property. In the course of bitter factional disputes, traditionalists as well as modernists laid claim to the heady prospects of boundless power in directing the architectural resources of the young Soviet state. During the rebuilding of the economy in the New Economic Policy

(NEP) period of the 1920s, it would appear that modernism in its various guises did indeed represent the future of Soviet architecture, particularly in Moscow.

Yet modernism was vulnerable on two seemingly contradictory counts: it emphasized the brilliance of individual architects (known among the Western avant-garde for their writings, project sketches, and relatively few completed projects), while at the same time modernist designs—particularly the housing projects, constructed within severely limited economic and technological constraints—seemed insufferably austere from a popular point of view. Both of these "defects" were resolutely addressed in the 1930s, as the grandomania of Stalinist planning imposed on urban construction a singleness of purpose that would have amazed prerevolutionary architects who had decried the lack of a unifying idea. (Certain of them, such as Ivan Fomin, were still active in the 1930s.) Like totalitarian architecture elsewhere in Europe during the interwar period, Stalinist architecture relied heavily on the hyperbolic application of traditional, often classical, elements in plans for boulevards and city squares on a superhuman scale, whereas the more innovative or rational uses of Western technology retreated to the obscurity of industrial architecture.

The pathos of an age tragically compounded of mass terror and heroic effort goes beyond the limits of this volume; but in its unremitting quest for monumentality, architecture during the 1930s and the decade following the Second World War was an indispensable part of the rhetoric of Stalinist industrialization and of "socialism in one country"—perhaps its most enduring expression. Such a course inevitably led to the public repudiation of the West; but although Soviet architectural journals fulminated against the West, they drew upon the opinions of American architects and planners such as Frank Lloyd Wright and Lewis Mumford to validate their sense of accomplishment. Only capitalist America, it seems, could provide an example of rapid industrialization on a scale comparable to that of the Soviet Union.

The superiority of the Soviet system was to be asserted in the culture of its urban landscape, which would avoid the horrors of the "imperialist city," even as it resembled the imperial city, Petersburg. To this end technology and innovation were subordinate to grandiose vistas and extravagant, proclamatory statements in building design, heedless of an impending crisis that would lead planners in the post-Stalinist period to dismiss architecture as style in favor of

standardized construction as social engineering. In a crowning irony, the very wastefulness and grandomania of Stalinist
architecture ensure its position as the last "age of architecture"
in the Soviet Union. Subsequent generations of architects—
often of considerable talent—have struggled to manage as
best they can the apparently insuperable problems of space
for housing and related services in cities such as Moscow and
Leningrad, while foreign firms are imported to build large
projects devoted primarily to a Western clientele in tourism
and international business.

★ ★ ★

Viewed from this perspective, it would seem that architecture in Russia (and the Soviet Union) during the twentieth
century has been subject to vicissitudes unmatched in this
century. Wars, revolutions, rapid industrialization, and the
imposition of a totalitarian regime and a command economy
have all left their mark on successive stages of development
in design and construction technology. The present volume,
which includes the work of four specialists in Russian architecture, represents a selective examination of the reshaping
of architecture as Russia moved into the modern age—from
capitalist boom to visions of a new social environment.

As Blair Ruble notes in the first chapter, the heroic scale
of imperial Petersburg seems a model of enlightened civic
concern in comparison to the almost unimaginable—and ultimately unrealized—scope of the 1936 design for a new urban
center in the south of Leningrad. The air of unreality characteristic of the competition sketches for the new square and
its surrounding buildings suggests a distant relation to Jean-
Baptiste Le Blond's first plans for Petersburg at the beginning
of the eighteenth century, whereas the project designs for the
Leningrad House of Soviets—including the winning entry
by Noi Trotskii—owe more than a passing debt to the German architect Peter Behrens. It was Behrens's design for the
German embassy in St. Petersburg (1911–12, on St. Isaac's
Square) that first provided an indication that architecture
could serve as an expression of state power in the twentieth
century.

In effect, Ruble's opening chapter provides both a frame
and a point of contrast for the developments discussed in this
study; for within the persistent demand on the part of certain
prerevolutionary architects and critics for a unified concept
of urban design based on traditional aesthetic values, there
also existed an open, experimental approach that had its own

visions of the future of Russian cities as cultural and financial centers. Despite the proximity of European modernism in architecture, American models for creating a new urban environment exerted considerable fascination on Russian observers, who saw a culture unencumbered by the past and possessed by a desire to develop the country's enormous resources. As described in Chapter 2, the often enthusiastic perceptions of America in the Russian architectural press may, in retrospect, be seen as overoptimistic or illusionary—particularly in regard to the possibilities of Russian development along American lines. Nonetheless, the visionary quality of so many of the commentaries on American architecture suggests a shared determination to achieve in tangible, architectural terms the manifest destinies of the two great powers of the twentieth century.

In Chapter 3 innovation and its obvious limits in Russian architecture at the beginning of the century are presented through the example of Moscow, with its often contradictory quest for both functionalism and a new aestheticism in architecture. Despite the atrophied development of basic services and the lack of an effective plan for regulating the city's growth, major construction projects during the three decades before the 1917 revolution created a new urban environment that survives throughout central Moscow to this day. At the same time, the rejection of the style moderne in Petersburg had its less militant counterpart in Moscow, where the exploration of color and plasticity in structural form yielded to a more austere tectonic logic couched in the idiom of neoclassicism.

If the financial and commercial needs of prerevolutionary Moscow produced apartment buildings, department stores, office buildings, and cultural institutions (such as the Museum of Fine Arts) funded largely by private sources, Blair Ruble's survey of modernist architecture in Moscow during the late 1920s and early 1930s demonstrates the transformation of both social structure and sources of support for new construction. Under the severe economic constraints of the time, Moscow and Leningrad functioned primarily within the built environment of the prerevolutionary period, while the new regime directed its attention toward buildings with a highly visible ideological and social function (workers' clubs, government institutions, newspaper headquarters, experimental housing projects). Despite the paucity of resources and the idealistic emphasis on communalism, one is impressed by the Russian avant-garde's use of architecture as a focus for the development of the individual—as opposed to the later uses of monumentality in the service of conformity and mass obedience to the will of the leader.

The fact that revolutionary enthusiasm and the dedication to radically innovative concepts of architecture far outpaced the reality of construction and available technology did little to hinder plans for the realization of the "fantasy of the mind." In Chapter 5, Milka Bliznakov describes the extent to which utopian visions of an architecture for a new society were extensively explored in literary works of science fiction, as well as in exhibits and journals sponsored by avant-garde architectural groups in the Soviet Union and their allies in Europe. In addition, new Soviet journals resumed the transfer of information on technology and major construction projects from European as well as American architectural and engineering periodicals—a process whose prerevolutionary antecedents are discussed in Chapter 2.

As the demands for industrialization stimulated an awareness of the available means to implement enormous projects in the real world, the advanced technology of the West provided hope for an unprecedented rate of growth on the part of a country still acutely aware of its lagging status among industrial powers. As Bliznakov points out, the work of foreign engineers was more highly valued than that of avant-garde architects (Soviet as well as European), whose idealistic theories concerning the role of architecture in the creation of a new social environment were increasingly discredited during the 1930s.

However, the visionary component of Russian utopian thought as applied to the architecture of the future was not a passing phenomenon, and it is telling that both Bliznakov and Anatole Kopp point to the significance of Nikolai Chernyshevskii's social utopian novel *What Is to Be Done?* (1863) in this regard. One might also note two other nineteenth-century Russian novels that contain visions of ideal cities of the future: the final chapter of Vladimir Sollogub's *Tarantas* (1845) and Vladimir Odoevskii's fantasy *The Year 4338,* which was written in the 1830s, but not published until 1926 (a very appropriate date in terms of Bliznakov's discussion). Even as certain of the more radical manifestations of visionary planning (such as deurbanization) were modified or discarded in the 1930s, the call for a rapid acceleration of Soviet development did not cease to exert a powerful influence on the imagination. Indeed, in the drive to overtake the future, the machinery of modern technology was invested with the status

7

of a cult, as illustrated in the films of Sergei Eisenstein (*The Old and the New*) and literary works such as Valentin Kataev's "documentary novel" *Time, Forward!* (1932, on the construction of the new steel mills in Magnitogorsk).

Bliznakov's discussion of the role of Western technology in the industrialization campaigns of the first two Five-Year Plans is amplified and expanded in detail by Anatole Kopp, who focuses on the reality of efforts to build a new order on the basis of heavy industry and describes the accomplishments as well as the frustrations of foreign architects and engineers at work in Stalin's Russia. The pragmatic idealism of German architects such as Ernst May, Bruno Taut, and Hannes Meyer was received with varying degrees of success, and Le Corbusier created a major landmark of the modernist movement in his Tsentrosoiuz project in Moscow. But it was the unpretentious industrial architecture of the Albert Kahn firm from Detroit that had the greatest impact on the industrialization campaign of the 1930s. Implemented on an enormous scale, the tractor plants and machine factories were not the stuff of utopian social visions; yet they played an indispensable role in the growth of heavy industry, which served the Soviet Union so effectively during the Second World War.

Kopp's description of Western architects who saw the Soviet Union as a land of advanced design, social idealism, and reconstruction (as well as a source of wages and profits during the Depression) should remind us that the relation between Russian architecture and the West has proceeded in both directions. Whereas Russian architects looked to the West for the means to implement futuristic visions or specific economic goals, European and American architects have been impressed by the apparently unlimited possibilities for construction and planning in the Soviet Union. It is appropriate that Kopp's chapter—and this volume—should conclude with another reference to visions of material utopia in Chernyshevskii's novel. The ambiguity of a visionary quest in a material world is inevitably left unresolved.

Does the dream of reshaping the built environment still exist in Soviet architecture? No doubt it does, yet it is equally certain that hopes of its realization have substantially declined after decades of standardized construction. Russian architects have rarely lacked for visions and ideals in the art of building, but deficiencies in the material base and the inability to build beyond the dictates of the construction bureaucracy have relegated these visions to the drawing board. Indeed, because of these constraints it seems that architecture will be the last area of artistic creativity in the Soviet Union to show the positive impact of *perestroika* and the loosening of central control. Perhaps architectural cooperatives will find opportunities to reestablish the all-important relation between architect and individual client; perhaps some of the more enterprising among contemporary architects will find commissions abroad. Whatever the particulars of the inevitable renascence of architecture in Russia (and the Soviet Union), Western architecture will continue to serve not simply as a source of new technology, but as a point of reference in setting a course toward the future.

1 FROM PALACE SQUARE TO MOSCOW SQUARE: ST. PETERSBURG'S CENTURY-LONG RETREAT FROM PUBLIC SPACE

Blair A. Ruble

URBAN space reveals much about the society that creates it; this is especially true of planned space where fundamental social relationships are consciously set in stone, concrete, steel, and glass.[1] Whereas shifting architectural and urban patterns reflect a society's adaptation to technological change, urban vistas express the manner in which societies function and think about themselves.[2] The later years of the nineteenth century and the early years of the twentieth witnessed a major transformation in the manner and materials of urban construction. Alternating waves of progressive and conservative stylistic responses to this transformation may be identified throughout the Western world—ranging from Ruskin-inspired picturesque to style moderne—as the Industrial Revolution produced a range of new building types (for example, the large factory, the railroad station, the commercial office building, the legislative center).[3]

The transfiguration of urban space in St. Petersburg/Leningrad during this period embodies the evolution of society-state relations in the wake of industrialization. This chapter will highlight the evolving nature of urban physical space during a period of rapid industrialization and technological change by comparing the ensemble of five central squares constructed between 1819 and 1859 with plans for a "New Petersburg" in the early years of the twentieth century and with the Moskovskii Prospekt project of 1936–41.[4]

FIVE CENTRAL SQUARES

Any exploration of the use of space in St. Petersburg should begin by acknowledging the emblematic significance of Peter I's creation. The city's symbolism as a "window on the West" was immediately understood when Peter declared his intention in 1703 to build a new capital. As architects and planners in the eighteenth and nineteenth centuries captured the pretensions of Peter and his successors, the resulting cityscape—impregnated with European ideas—remained for decades essentially a haphazard Russian town behind the orderly facades of public buildings.[5] Imperial planners counted on a network of central squares to eradicate some of these enduring vestiges of Russian *bezobraziia* (meaning "ugliness" in this context) that had marred officials' vistas for over a century.[6]

Catherine II and her progeny, considering themselves rulers of a major European power, commissioned architects who drew on a sober neoclassicism then popular in France to express their majesty and European spirit. Under Catherine, the Neva delta's silty banks were encased with granite, while her Commission for the Masonry Construction of St. Petersburg and Moscow struggled to create blocklong facades out of the varied buildings facing this riverfront with its new aristocratic image.[7] The river's newfound grandeur unified the city's previ-

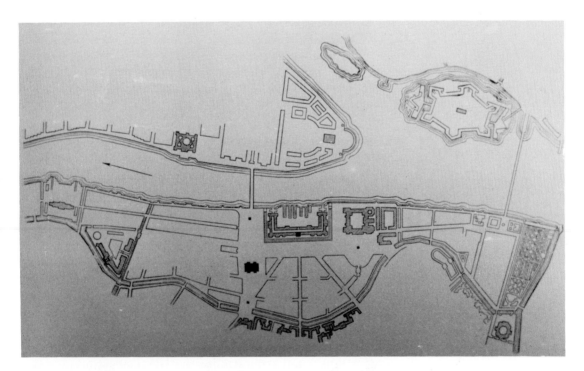

Map 1   Ensemble of the central squares of Petersburg, with the embankments of the Neva and Moika. From Iu. A. Egorov, *Ansambl' v gradostroitel'stve SSSR.*

ously scattered parts, for the Neva embankment came to serve as a stone ribbon binding the capital together.[8]

No effort was spared during Catherine's reign to make the capital more magnificent and beautiful. Comprehensive city plans projected a central core of significant buildings positioned around squares, with each structure retaining a modicum of individuality, yet blending into a sweeping ensemble. Architects were confined primarily to the design of a few well-situated monumental buildings around the city, whereas surrounding areas were left to later generations to complete. This task of realizing Catherine's classical masterpiece eventually fell to her somber son Paul I and to her two grandsons, Alexander I and Nicholas I.

The capital blossomed as the Old Regime gathered strength. From the time Catherine died in 1796 until Alexander's death in 1825, St. Petersburg added 20 percent more territory to the city limits and nearly doubled in population to around 420,000 residents.[9] Enormous construction projects mushroomed as three- and four-story structures replaced the old one- and two-story ones. Between 1806 and 1823 Adrian Zakharov redesigned the Admiralty and its central spire—perhaps the city's most visible landmark—and thus strengthened the power of the tri-radial street pattern established during the reign of Empress Anna (Figs. 1, 2). Other major projects of the period included completion of Tomas de Thomon's Exchange (1805–10) on the prominent point of Vasilevskii Island (Fig. 3), construction of Andrei Voronikhin's Mining Institute (1806–11) intended to anchor the western terminus of the Vasilevskii Island riverfront (Fig. 4), and the initiation between 1801 and the 1850s of a beautification plan for the Nevskii Prospekt (Fig. 5). Five new central squares, surrounding the Admiralty and built between 1819 and 1859, completed this extraordinarily ambitious attempt at planned city building.[10] Early nineteenth-century St. Petersburg thus came to reflect the confidence of an Alexandrine empire flush from military victory over Napoleon. The system of five interpenetrating central squares began at the Winter Palace to the east and extended past the Admiralty to St. Isaac's Cathedral to the west. The Palace, Razvodnaia, Admiralty, Senate, and St. Isaac's squares merged into a single urban system (Fig. 6).

Palace Square had remained an unsolved architectural puzzle for almost half a century. Imperial demands for ceremonial majesty competed with an irregular site hemmed in by the unconnected remnants of a complex street plan, the serpen-

2 Admiralty. St. Petersburg. Pediment detail.
Photo: William Brumfield.

3 Stock Exchange. St. Petersburg. 1805–10. Architect: Jean Thomas de Thomon. Photo: William Brumfield.

4 Mining Institute. St. Petersburg. 1806–11. Architect: Andrei Voronikhin. Photo: William Brumfield.

5 Moika Canal, view toward Nevskii Prospekt and the Stroganov Palace. Architect: Bartolomeo Rastrelli. On right, Building of the General Staff. Architect: Carlo Rossi. (See also Figure 7.) Photo: William Brumfield.

tine meandering of the Moika River, and the outward embankments of the Admiralty's scruffy shipyards.[11] In 1819, the Commission for the Development of the Square Opposite the Winter Palace recommended the creation of an irregular, almost semicircular plaza unique in a city of rectangular spaces. Such an unusual opening in the street plan had been suggested by the already existing buildings, though the hodgepodge nature of these structures somewhat obscured the felicitousness of this approach.[12] Carlo Rossi—the predominant architect of the Alexandrine era—won the commission to complete the new square, designing the starkly elegant General Staff Building (1819–29) to set off the baroque exuberance of the palace itself. The Alexander Column, designed by Auguste Montferrand and erected in 1827, bound the conflicting styles together by providing a focal point at the square's center (Fig. 7).

Immediately to the west of Palace Square, fortifications and moats were taken down during Zakharov's redesign of the Admiralty, thus opening up Razvodnaia Square fronting onto the Neva between the Winter Palace and the Admiralty and expanding a kilometer-long belt of open space—Admiralty Square—all the way to the Royal Guards Riding Academy (Manezh) beyond.[13] Admiralty Square developed as the lynchpin of an urban system uniting the radial avenues of Anna's time and the emerging central square system of Alexander I. Its visual impact was reduced in the early 1870s with the planting of trees throughout the square, as can be seen today in the Alexander Garden that replaced it.

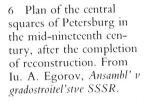

6 Plan of the central squares of Petersburg in the mid-nineteenth century, after the completion of reconstruction. From Iu. A. Egorov, *Ansambl' v gradostroitel'stve SSSR*.

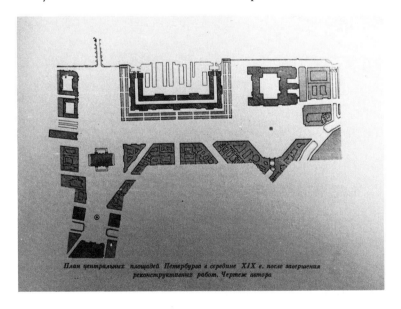

План центральных площадей Петербурга в середине XIX в. после завершения реконструктивных работ. Чертеж автора

Imperial architects had less success in designing the Senate
and St. Isaac's squares to the west. In 1827 Nicholas I ordered
the reconstruction of the Senate Building.[14] By 1829 Rossi
had won a competition with a design that called for a united
facade extending the entire length of the western side of the
Senate Square from the Riding Academy to the riverbank.
In order to balance the western wing of the Admiralty across
the square, the Holy Synod agreed to Rossi's plan to construct
its new building adjacent to that of the Senate. Rossi designed
a unified facade for the overall ensemble tied together by a
central ceremonial archway over a small street separating the
two structures (Fig. 8). The combined Senate and Synod
buildings (1829–34) succeeded through Rossi's use of ornamentation to obscure differences in the elevation and size of
each building, and through a gentle curve in the Synod complex that permits the square to flow gently on to the Neva
embankment.

In contrast to Rossi's masterpiece, Auguste Montferrand's
ponderous St. Isaac's Cathedral (1819–59) dominated
the nineteenth-century city and continues to overwhelm its
own square as well as that of the Senate (Figs. 9, 10). The

7 Palace Square and
Building of the General
Staff. St. Petersburg.
1819–29. Architect: Carlo
Rossi. Photo: William
Brumfield.

subject of much controversy and intrigue during design and construction, St. Isaac's became a product of committee deliberation and imperial intervention. The finished building offered an inharmonious addition to its surroundings in both style and scale—a situation that was not improved by the construction of the nondescript Mariinskii Palace (1839–45) on the opposite side of St. Isaac's Square. Designed by Andrei Shtakenshneider, the palace was soon rejected as an imperial dwelling, and it subsequently housed the Imperial State Council. Despite its aesthetic deficiencies, the building of the Mariinskii Palace completed the city's system of five central squares, and with it Petersburg's century of grand urban design.[15]

The central squares integrated 478,400 square yards of urban space into a united system that dominated Petersburg's life for a century.[16] They contain within their sweep nearly all of the essential institutions of the monarchy, government,

8 The Senate and Holy Synod. St. Petersburg. 1829–34. Architect: Carlo Rossi. Photo: William Brumfield.

9 Cathedral of St. Isaac. St. Petersburg. 1819–59. Architect: Auguste Mont-ferrand. North facade. Photo: William Brumfield.

10 Cathedral of St. Isaac. West facade. Photo: William Brumfield.

state religion, and municipal administration, including the Winter Palace; the Imperial State Council; the Senate; the General Staff Building; the Admiralty; the Royal Guards Regiment Staff Building and Riding Academy; the Ministries of Foreign Affairs, Finance, Agriculture, and State Property; the Holy Synod; St. Isaac's Cathedral; and the Palace of the Governor of St. Petersburg. Nevskii Prospekt, the city's main commercial thoroughfare, began at the squares and was dominated by the Admiralty Tower at its northern terminus. The Nevskii itself was being rebuilt during this period, so that a brief walk along it from the Admiralty would bring one to Voronikhin's Kazan Cathedral (1801–11) (Fig. 11), Rossi's Mikhailovskii Palace (1819–40) on the Arts Square, and his Aleksandrinskii Drama Theater (1828–32) with its connecting Theater Street—neoclassical masterpieces all.

Petersburg's five central squares established a pleasing sequence of alternating closed and open spaces throughout the very heart of the imperial capital. Some individual squares—especially Palace Square—came to serve as outdoor rooms, each retaining a defined sense of place.[17] The irregularities of the sites combined with variations in style over the six

11   Cathedral of the Kazan Mother of God. St. Petersburg. 1801–11. Architect: Andrei Voronikhin. Photo: William Brumfield.

decades of construction—witness the baroque Winter Palace
and the neoclassical General Staff Building staring at one
another past the Alexander Column—to reduce the tedium
of overambitious symmetry.[18] Each square was enlivened, in
turn, by the radial avenues that channeled the life of the streets
into them and strengthened the role of the squares as the heart
of the city.[19] For an essentially neoclassical ensemble, the end
result is rather unexpected: a sense of spontaneity and public
activity as one moves through each of the squares in succes-
sion. As Michael Berman has observed, "In generations to
come, Petersburg's common people would gradually find
ways to make their presence felt, to make the city's great
spaces and structures their own."[20]

Almost a century ago, Camillo Sitte demonstrated how
plazas serve as well-appointed and richly furnished main halls
for a city, enhancing and enriching public life.[21] From what
we know of the physical setting of Petersburg's five central
squares, and bearing in mind Sitte's perceptive observations,
we should not be surprised to discover that the five squares
were the site of nearly every major event in the city's history
since the reign of Alexander I, including at least four revolutions,[22] scores of unofficial demonstrations, and hundreds
of official ceremonies (imperial as well as socialist). And this
is not to mention the occasional rock concert or go-cart race.
In providing a suitable stage for their own public ceremonies,
the Romanov emperors provided an identity for the city as
a whole. Imperial ceremonial space became public space, even
as nineteenth-century European architectural taste began to
emphasize the private realm over the public.[23] Petersburg's
aristocratic public order gave way to an inward-looking private culture only after peasants flocking to local factories had
inundated the city's streets.

NEW PETERSBURG

In his novel set in St. Petersburg on the eve of the First World
War, Andrei Bely wrote:

A ring of many-chimneyed factories girded St. Petersburg. . . .
   In the morning the great human swarm crept toward them; the
streets of the suburbs crawled with this moving horde. In those
days, there was no lack of agitation in the factories; the workers
had become garrulous; Brownings circulated among them, and
something else. . . .
   This agitation, which ringed St. Petersburg, had penetrated into

the very heart of the city. It had first gripped the Islands, then rushed headlong across the Liteiny and Nikolaevsky bridges; on the Nevsky Prospekt, it assumed a human polypedal form, and this polypedal swarm changed constantly as it circulated along the Prospekt; an observer might have noted the black shaggy cap from the blood-soaked fields of Manchuria; the number of passing cylinder hats was diminished correspondingly; and the air carried the turbulent shouts of anti-Government urchins who were distributing revolutionary leaflets between the railway station and the Admiralty.[24]

The scene described by Bely is the city that Alexander I's Petersburg eventually became. The transformation of the elegant classicism, the cavalry boots, and cylinder hats of the Alexandrine capital to the squalor and despair, the polypedal swarms, and the shaggy black caps of Bely's city represents a profound change closely linked to industrialization and to the social forces it unleashed. To appreciate how the city was being shaped as the nineteenth century continued, it became less important to understand the taste of the tsar and of his favorite architects than to comprehend the social realities facing the hundreds of thousands of peasants who moved to St. Petersburg and began to become workers.

The omnipresent order of the city at the beginning of the nineteenth century faded, with the result that as the twentieth century began, St. Petersburg had become the most expensive and least healthy capital in Europe. With a mortality rate high even by urban Russian standards, the capital suffered from fierce epidemics of infectious diseases brought about in part by geography (the city's position in the middle of a swamp) and in part by municipal ineptitude (the city's woefully inadequate water and sewerage systems). In addition, St. Petersburg experienced pronounced social inequality, frequent epidemics of venereal disease, a high incidence of drunkenness, a soaring crime rate, abysmal housing conditions (10 percent of the population lived in so-called *ugol,* or "corner habitation"), and high levels of illiteracy (31 percent of the population in 1910).[25] Reviewing various social indicators, James Bater concluded that "few places were ever so hazardous to live in" as turn-of-the-century St. Petersburg.[26]

Behind the facades created by Catherine II, Alexander I, and Nicholas I, numerous social cancers grew unabated as the process of industrialization gradually converted the aristocratic city of Catherine and her grandsons into a city of capitalists, merchants, and peasants in worker's clothing. St. Petersburg had always been home to industry; and as its industries grew, so did its financial institutions.[27] From the time of the founding of the State Bank in 1860 until 1914, the number of banking establishments grew to more than four dozen.[28] The emergence of joint stock companies and commodities exchanges, as well as the arrival of large-scale foreign investment similarly added to the importance of St. Petersburg as a financial center.

For the urban environment, these fundamental alterations in the shape of the local economy had one primary impact: overcrowding. From 1870 until 1914, 1,500,000 new residents moved to the city, including 1,000,000 arrivals after 1890 and 350,000 in the boom years between 1908 and 1913 alone.[29] This influx of people coincided with a reduction in population controls that had previously inhibited migration from the countryside to the city. As late as midcentury, the labor supply of St. Petersburg Province (*guberniia*) remained essentially urban in background. This soon changed. By the 1910s, the Russian capital was the fifth largest in Europe, surpassed only by London, Paris, Vienna, and Berlin. Both its population and its employment structures were dominated by businessmen and workers, many of whom were fresh from the countryside. Imperial image notwithstanding, St. Petersburg had become a city of peasants.

The pressures of industrialization coincided with a rapidly escalating population to overwhelm municipal administrators. Housing and zoning codes were largely ignored, demand far outstripped the supply of municipal services, and the city's severe climate made a bad situation worse. The causes of the near total collapse of municipal administration during the last quarter of the nineteenth century were cultural, structural, and financial in character. The cultural roots of this collapse lay in society's fundamentally pre-urban outlook. For the nobility, St. Petersburg was the place to go for the winter social season; for the peasant, it was a place to go to earn money for the family back home. Many workers returned to the fields when the harvest was ready. Such low levels of commitment to the city combined with an autocratic administrative system to force municipal officials to become more concerned with the needs of the monarch than with those of the politically passive populace. The city's underdeveloped municipal institutions retained an essentially static view of their mission in a quickly changing world.

These cultural determinants were closely linked to structural problems. Nicholas I's municipal reforms of 1846 firmly tied city authorities to the tsar. By the late 1860s, for example, police responsibilities fell to the national interior ministry. Moreover, city officials frequently lacked authority to implement municipal laws. As early as 1833, the city had attempted to initiate zoning restrictions regulating some of the more disturbing industrial processes. These rules failed to protect city neighborhoods from the sights and smells of industrialization. Repeated efforts in 1879, 1905, and 1913 to control factory location similarly proved unsuccessful.

In many ways, the primary reasons underlying the municipal authorities' seeming inaction were financial. The city's operating budget remained modest by European and even by Russian standards of the day, being drawn largely from profits generated by such municipal concessions as the tram system, the water system, the gas works, and a municipal slaughterhouse.[30] Under constant inflationary pressure, the city government eventually was forced to seek additional funds through the London and Paris bond markets. Small by the practice of the period, the charges for servicing this municipal debt nonetheless tripled between 1901 and 1910 to 2.9 million rubles annually.[31] In the end, the underdeveloped and underfinanced municipal structure proved incapable of coping with the changes brought by industrialization. St. Petersburg emerged as a symbol of yet another Western phenomenon: urban revolution.

Many Petersburgers deplored the transformation of their capital from the relative order of Nicholas I to the growing chaos of Nicholas II. As the industrial revolution swept the Russian empire, the capital's intellectual and cultural elites embraced at times antithetical nationalist and internationalist concepts. Slavophile nationalism found expression in various attempts to define the Russian national character. In architecture, this movement shared broad concerns with the emergence throughout Europe of a romantic interest in the past. As in Europe, this process of discovery took place in reverse chronological order and led to extensive eclecticism which, in St. Petersburg, added to the destruction of the city's neoclassical spirit (Figs. 12, 13). The Church of the Resurrection of the Savior on the Blood (1883–1907) on the site of Alexander II's assassination provides the best St. Petersburg example of efforts to recreate a distinctive national Russian architectural form.[32]

Against this romantic Russian national revival were posed the overtly internationalist stances of the journal *Mir iskusstva*

(World of art, 1898–1904) and of its successors *Starye gody* (The old years, 1907–16), *Zolotoe runo* (The golden fleece, 1906–9), and *Apollon* (1909–17). As part of a cosmopolitan symbolist movement of the 1890s, such groups remained concentrated in the more Western-oriented capital and were attracted to the past of their own city. The neoclassicism of Catherine II and Alexander I held particular fascination, as can be seen in the works of the brothers Benois—Leontii and Aleksandr—and in Ivan Fomin's grandiose proposal in 1912 for a "New Petersburg" on Golodai Island that was to emulate the classical style and grand scale of the first Petersburg.[33]

New Petersburg was envisioned as an entire region built to recapture the spirit of a mythical old Petersburg that had been torn asunder by industrialization.[34] Considerable imagination must be used when examining Fomin's sketches and plans to discern what the new city would have been like (Fig. 14). The project's scale evidently was to have been enormous,

12 Mutual Land Credit Society building. Admiralty Quay, St. Petersburg. 1877–80. Architects: Georg Krakau, Nikolai Benois. Constructed on the Neva embankment in front of Adrian Zakharov's Admiralty, this building is a prime example of the city's disregard for its classical heritage during the latter part of the nineteenth century. Photo: William Brumfield.

with pedestrians appearing as small ink splotches against a ponderous neoclassical backdrop. Traditional Petersburg classicism was to combine with new building technologies to produce a complex dwarfing even the formidable central squares of a half-century before. It is difficult to imagine any of Fomin's snow-blown spaces functioning as a room for the city, as did Palace Square. Rather, the messy refuse of industrialization was to be contained within bleak, flat, symmetrical, perfectly balanced, column-lined apartment houses, sterile streets, and plazas. No room was available here for a baroque palace, a quirky twisting canal, or even a perfectly balanced general staff building. Life would need to retreat

13 Apartment building. Admiralty Quay, St. Petersburg. 1880s. Architect: A. Kolb. Photo: William Brumfield.

from the streets into the privacy of whatever rooms would be built behind these grave facades. The aim of the day was to regain order. Fomin's New Petersburg would have asserted that order even as Petersburg society itself was falling apart.

Though never built, New Petersburg reveals an impulse on the part of "proper" society to turn back the rabble in the street. This withdrawal from the street signals an erosion of public life—and a growing preoccupation with the private realm—that was occurring elsewhere in Europe at the time.[35] It also presaged the ultimate victory of the private realm over the public under the auspices of the nominally communalistic socialist regime that was to follow.

MOSKOVSKII PROSPEKT

Prerevolutionary reactions to the disintegration of the urban fabric brought about by industrialization remained salient following the Bolshevik seizure of power of November 7 (October 25), 1917. Within weeks of assuming power, the Bolsheviks removed their capital from Petrograd (as the city had been known since the early days of the First World War) to safer quarters in Moscow. Following their consolidation of power through a bloody civil war, a wave of "revolutionary" currents swept Russia. As S. Frederick Starr has argued, such movements in urban planning were inexorably bound to debates begun well before 1917.[36] Two basic responses were posed to the urban malaise of prerevolutionary Russia. The first was essentially a "Red" variant of the an-

14 Sketch of the main square of "New Petersburg." Architect: Ivan Fomin. Published in *Ezhegodnik obshchestva arkhitektorov-khudozhnikov* (Annual of the Society of Architect-Artists [*EOAK*]), 1913.

tiurban ideal of the Garden City Movement that had been launched in England by the appearance in 1898 of Ebenezer Howard's *Tomorrow: A Peaceful Path to Reform*. The second was "classical" in that it found answers to Soviet Russia's inherited neoclassical forms. The classicism of the "New Urbanism" of the brothers Benois and of Ivan Fomin sought urban and planning strategies that dismissed private property, demanded large-scale state intervention, and produced a style characterized by grandeur and unity. By the end of the 1920s, with a new cult of the state emerging, the fundamental characteristics of the Petrine-Catherinian-Alexandrine tradition as translated by the *Mir iskusstva* movement of the 1890s and early 1900s had become the foundation of a new Stalinist urban ethos. The Moskovskii Prospekt project of the late 1930s resolved some of the multiple tensions between society and state in favor of the state.

The years of the first Five-Year Plan (1928–32) witnessed a tidal wave of peasants fleeing the countryside for the cities, Leningrad included.[37] Although Leningrad declined somewhat in population during the civil war years, it had passed the million population mark by 1923, and by 1931, more than 2.5 million were residing in the city.[38] Consequently, Leningrad, like nearly every Soviet city of any consequence, was in chaos. In 1931, Stalin's leading troubleshooter, Lazar Kaganovich, brought an end to the anti-city experiments of the 1920s with the declaration that the Soviet future would be urban.[39] The state quickly moved to control architectural and urban design with traditional statist neoclassicism emerging as the accepted style. Kaganovich's views had pivotal consequences for the future of Soviet urban planning. Kaganovich proclaimed the primacy of economic considerations in urban planning and administration. Denying the feasibility of a radical urban transformation, Kaganovich openly scorned the view that the city was inherently capitalist and innately evil. Moreover, the preeminence of industrial concerns in his directives deemphasized architectural planning and, instead, favored economic planning.[40] This accent combined with a Stalinist predilection for grandeur to generate a classical historicism devoid of human feeling.

By the beginning of the second Five-Year Plan (1932–36), the architectural planning process had become focused on housing, public buildings, and aesthetics. As early as 1922, the Scientific Bureau of Urban Planning (Nauchnoe biuro gradostroitelstva) had been established in Leningrad to centralize the city's planning.[41] By 1928, the first formal national planning organization—the Union of Architects-Urbanists (ARU)—was founded. The ARU proved to be the first step in a concerted policy of subjugating numerous conflicting organizations and viewpoints to a united official policy.

The tendency toward centralization accelerated throughout the first Five-Year Plan as Giprogor, the first national urban planning agency, began operations in 1930.[42] By 1933, all architectural and planning efforts were unified within a national network for civil (*Gorstroiproekt*) and industrial (*Promstroiproekt*) institutions. A year later, the Communist Party helped to organize the Academy of Architects of the USSR and the Union of Soviet Architects, thereby placing the professional and organizational life of all Soviet architects and planners under central control. The First All-Union Conference on Construction, convened in December 1935, ratified this centralization of the urban planning and architectural professions.[43]

The impact of these developments was not totally negative. Cities—Leningrad in particular—benefited from renewed official support once the Soviet future was declared to be predominantly urban. Kaganovich's proclamation, for example, set in motion activities that eventually resulted in promulgation of a new citywide plan for Leningrad.

In August 1935, the Central Committee of the All-Union Communist Party (Bolshevik), the USSR Council of People's Commissars, the Leningrad City Party Committee, and the Leningrad City Soviet jointly proclaimed resolutions leading to the final enactment of a general development plan for Leningrad to take effect in 1936.[44] According to the plan drawn up under the direction of Lev Ilin and Vladimir Vitman, the historic city core around the Admiralty and Neva was to be abandoned for a new and grander center along the sixty-meter-wide International (now Moskovskii) Prospekt running directly south for ten kilometers from Peace Square (Fig. 15).[45] The route paralleled the city's major nineteenth-century rail lines and had served from time to time as a major entry into the city. The Konstantin Military School (1809), Technological Institute (1831), and Moscow Victory Gates (1834–38), commemorating the defeat of Napoleon in 1812, were all located along the proposed route of the new Moskovskii Prospekt.[46] The focal point of the new center was to be a gargantuan House of Soviets strategically placed along the thoroughfare.

In March 1936, city officials requested designs for the House of Soviets. During the previous decade, district houses of soviets had been commissioned throughout the city. Together with palaces of culture (such as Aleksandr Gegello and David Krichevskii's Gorky Palace of Culture [1927] and Noi Trotskii and Solomon Kozak's Kirov Palace of Culture [1930–37]) and educational institutions (such as Aleksandr Nikolskii's Tenth Anniversary of October School on Tractor Street [1930]), the houses of soviets were among the few outlets for more radical architectural design in the classicism-

15   Project of a new system for a city center in Leningrad. Architect: N. V. Baranov. Published in *Arkhitektura Leningrada*, 1941.

obsessed city—as is evident in Noi Trotskii's Kirov District Soviet Building (1931–34) and Valerian Daugul and Ivan Fomin's Moscow District Soviet Building (1935). Over time, the designs for the district houses of soviets had become more conservative, such as Ivan Fomin, G. Gedike, and Evgenii Levinson's Nevskii District House of Soviets (1937–40). Indeed, after the war the Kuibyshev district soviet assumed residence in the renovated Beloselskii-Belozerskii Palace on Nevskii Prospekt.[47]

The competition guidelines for the citywide House of Soviets on Moskovskii Prospekt called for a structure 230 to
260 meters long, 120 to 150 meters deep, and 5 to 7 stories
tall to be built "in the region of the Elektrosila Factory."[48]
The competition also requested plans for a ceremonial square
with seating for 8,000 spectators surrounded by the House
of Soviets, a new "bolshoi" theater, a palace of youth, and
a house of the Red Army and Navy. The city government
requested that the plans for the House of Soviets include
provisions for proper facilities for regional and city party,
government, and Young Communist League (Komsomol)
councils and committees, as well as for a 3,000-seat auditorium and a library housing 100,000 volumes. Constructed
between 1936 and 1941, the winning proposal by Noi Trotskii, Ia. N. Lukina, and Iakov Svirskii proved to be somewhat
smaller than the structure proposed by the competition.[49]
Nevertheless, the House of Soviets remained a leviathan
structure. Running 220 meters long, 150 meters deep, and
up to 8 stories high, the building faced a square 200 meters
long by 400 meters wide, with seating facilities for 2,500 to
3,000 spectators (Figs. 16, 17, 18).

Noi Trotskii's own description of the project provides an
insight into the preoccupation with monumentality during
the most repressive years of Stalin's rule:

It is difficult to determine one or another style as the model for the
House of Soviets. Undoubtedly it is linked with the architectural

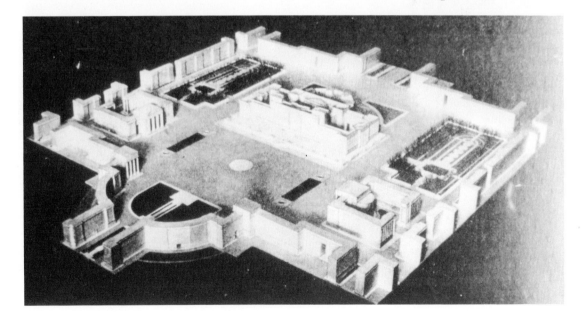

16 Project model for the
construction of a public
square and House of Sovi-
ets. Leningrad. Architect:
Noi Trotskii. *Arkhitektura
Leningrada*, 1937.

traditions of our city, and to an obvious degree it has its native sources. However, the uniquely tense rhythm of the entire building, the laconic approach to the treatment of details, and the basic mass, its scale—all these significantly distinguish the House of Soviets from all previous architecture and place it within the ranks of contemporary buildings.[50]

Commenting on the difficulties in designing the facade of such a massive structure, Trotskii noted: "A certain monot-

17 Model for House of Soviets. Leningrad. Architect: Noi Trotskii. *Arkhitektura Leningrada*, 1937.

18 Plan of Leningrad House of Soviets. *Arkhitektura Leningrada*, 1937.

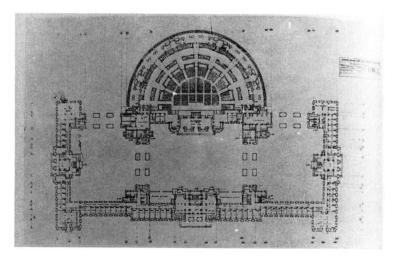

32

ony in the twenty-two-column portico [!] is broken in the
final version by the introduction of two pylons, worked in
rich relief, into the row of columns, and by a more complicated rhythm in the placement of the columns (in the middle
part the columns are paired)."[51] Bartolomeo Rastrelli, builder
of the Winter Palace, would have sympathized. Yet Trotskii
was interested not only in discussing aesthetic matters, but
also in defining the building's political role:

Having in this manner defused the monotony of the portico, one
also defines and fixes the position for the state shield on top, which
is linked with the sculptural frieze and with the monument to
V. I. Lenin. . . .
    The sculptural frieze, crowning the central colonnade, . . . por-
trays from one side the stages in socialist construction, and from
the other, characteristic moments in the defense of the country [Fig.
19]. The state shield (eleven meters square) is projected to be cast
in bronze, with the introduction of luminescent semiprecious stones
in the outlines of the hammer and sickle and the star.[52]

On the interior, the uses of monumentality were indulged
with equal enthusiasm, particularly in the design of the main
Assembly Hall (Figs. 20, 21). Again, Trotskii's measured description provides the best catalog of extravagance:

The Assembly Hall is designed in a monumental style and with a
major classical order. The amphitheater culminates in a row of

19 Sketch of main facade
of Leningrad House of So-
viets. *Arkhitektura Leningrada*, 1937.

33

doubled shafts and pylons, which bear the weight of the auditorium ceiling and the galleries. Niches in the pylons contain statues of heroic people in our Soviet Union—a pilot, a sailor, a worker, and a kolkhoznik. The portal, in which the tribunal of the presidium is placed, represents the architectural continuation and culmination of the hall [Fig. 22]. In the center of the presidium is an enormous bust of V. I. Lenin. Behind the presidium, in galleries, is a space for the orchestra.[53]

20   Sketch of east facade of Leningrad House of Soviets, with main Assembly Hall. *Arkhitektura Leningrada*, 1937.

The above passages are only a small fragment in Trotskii's recital of magnificence, which was even more lavishly displayed in the main dining room (Fig. 23). But in terms of the great tradition of public space in this city, the most sig-

22 Sketch of presidium tribunal, main Assembly Hall, Leningrad House of Soviets. *Arkhitektura Leningrada*, 1937.

23 Sketch of dining room, Leningrad House of Soviets. *Arkhitektura Leningrada*, 1937.

21 (facing page, bottom) Interior sketch of main Assembly Hall, Leningrad House of Soviets; 3,000-seat capacity. *Arkhitektura Leningrada*, 1937.

nificant point concerns the way in which the monstrous building of the House of Soviets had already overwhelmed the still vacant territory surrounding it.

Despite rapid progress made on the construction of the House of Soviets, Leningrad city administrators came to view the initial general plan as impractical. In 1938, a team of architects under Nikolai Baranov and Aleksandr Naumov revised the original plan yet again in an effort to make more effective use of the available land.[54] The projected city population remained at 3.5 million, but the total territory of urban development covered by the plan decreased from 216 to 181 square miles. Moreover, the House of Soviets project was pared down to cover a total of about 4.5 acres instead of more than 16. Baranov later observed that this reduction brought the planned ensemble into scale with such monumental urban networks as the Mall in Washington, D.C., and the Champs-Elysees in Paris.[55] The new plan also noted "serious inconveniences" resulting from an immediate abandonment of the historic city center.

Three factors contributed to the planners' preoccupation with moving the city's population southward. First, the new center was designed to supersede the historic city core. Second, the projected move to the south sought an end to the city's tragic pattern of flooding by shifting the population to higher ground. Third, once the decision was made to abandon the historic city center, the move to the south became inevitable. With the Finnish border less than twenty-five miles to the north, national security interests demanded urban development in the opposite direction. The short but bloody Winter War with the Finns in 1939–40 demonstrated the military wisdom of such a plan, for Leningrad was quickly transformed into a garrison city.[56]

The Moskovskii Prospekt project was said to draw on traditional Petersburg extended facades. The House of Soviets and the other buildings surrounding Moscow Square, however, were not united ensembles so much as isolated, separate, freely articulated solids that competed with one another for public attention.[57] Public space—and with it, public life—became a residue rather than an objective. New technologies helped create this new environment, of course, because they permitted construction on a scale unimaginable to Zakharov, Voronikhin, and Rossi. More was happening than simply an expansion of scale, for spontaneity and a sense of place were also lost. The endless linear avenue with its anomic outcroppings of parks and squares here and there served as a thoroughfare from one place to another rather than a place in and of itself.[58] Communal gatherings became isolated public spectacles cut off from the life of the city and viewed from grandstands rather than spontaneous events integral to the urban experience. Building and citizen alike grew isolated, while state authority was glorified (Fig. 24).

POSTWAR RECONSTRUCTION

In the early morning hours of June 22, 1941, the German army crashed across the Polish frontier into the Soviet Union; on September 17, forward elements of the *Wehrmacht* captured the southern terminus of the Leningrad streetcar system. In concert with the Finns—who were seeking recovery of territories lost just two years before—the Germans prepared for a final assault that never came. On September 25, Hitler began to shift troops to the Moscow front in an effort to drive the Soviet government from its capital. The Germans and Finns surrounding Leningrad dug in, and the city's nine hundred days of horror began.[59] The blockade of Leningrad lasted twenty-eight months until January 27, 1944. During this period, an estimated one million Leningraders perished.[60] In addition to the human loss, much of the city's capital plant was obliterated by direct attack, civilian scavenging, and abandonment.

In 1944, with the city liberated but in shambles, the USSR State Defense Committee announced a plan for rebuilding Leningrad.[61] Recognizing that the population had fought and

24 Sketch of Leningrad House of Soviets and main square, with masses marching past statue of Lenin. *Arkhitektura Leningrada*, 1937.

37

died for "Piter," the resulting city plan reasserted the primacy of the city's historic center. Starting in 1945–46, more than 700 million rubles were invested in the city's reconstruction efforts.[62] The 1950 dedication of the 100,000-seat Kirov Stadium (1932–50) designed by Aleksandr Nikolskii and others for Krestovskii Island marked the culmination of the reconstruction period.[63] By choosing to preserve the city's historic center, postwar planners favored an alternative model of urban development over that which had dominated the 1930s. Eventually, this model would lend support to the attempt to regain a more public urban face in the 1970s and 1980s.[64]

St. Petersburg's century-long retreat from the public realm was completed in Leningrad's Moscow Square. Thomas Bender has observed that it is a city's public life, and not its economic function or level of industrialization, that differentiates the urban experience.[65] The life of the streets and other public places generates a public culture that requires the space for making, inscribing, and interpreting public experiences. The technologies of the twentieth century together with the Stalinist ethos of the State permitted the most oppressive elements of pseudoclassicism a free reign in Leningrad. These forces undermined the harmony and balance of public spaces that had provided an arena for public life in the city. By the outbreak of the Second World War, Leningrad had managed to combine the excesses of statist pseudoclassicism with those of the modern era.

As Moskovskii Prospekt began to take shape, a series of grand individual buildings were scattered across the cityscape. What mattered to the Leningrad architects of the 1930s and to their state patrons was that each building should impose itself on the passerby and on its surroundings. This objective was perhaps more apparent during the 1930s and 1940s than it is today, for much of the land to each side of Moskovskii Prospekt initially remained vacant. In any case, the classic united facade was lost, because the broad ten-kilometer sweep of Moskovskii Prospekt never integrated its individual parts into a broader urban context as had the five central squares of a century before, which had served as the starting point for the city's central street plan. The world of the private realm—the concealed life taking place inside these buildings—became more important than any desire to provide a public space for human interaction.

Such modernist excesses would become more stark elsewhere following the Second World War. They were disguised along Moskovskii Prospekt by heroic columns and grand balconies covering steel skeletons. Nevertheless, just as elsewhere in the industrial world, Soviet society was turning in on itself by midcentury. This reversal was visible in the very material of its cities.

Caution is advised, of course, in any attempt to evaluate urban space in isolation from the society producing it. Still, the evolution of urban space over time frequently exposes that society's sense of self. In St. Petersburg, the continuing vigor of communalism of the imperial period in Russia was heightened by ceremonial ensembles intended to present the tsar to the public. The enforced anomie of Stalinist urban planning similarly revealed a general turning away from community in a nominally communal society. In conclusion, an examination of these three major planning projects in St. Petersburg/Leningrad over a century of rapid technological change illuminates some of the broader contours of the sweeping social transformations that were occurring within the urban environment.

NOTES

1. I would like to take this opportunity to express my gratitude to Theodore C. Bestor, author of *Neighborhood Tokyo* (Stanford: Stanford University Press, 1989), who has helped me to experience and appreciate urban space with greater understanding.

2. For further exposition of this observation, see the essays in Anthony D. King, ed., *Buildings and Society* (Boston: Routledge & Kegan Paul, 1980).

3. For a particularly informative discussion of these changes, see Robert Macleod, *Style and Society: Architectural Ideology in Britain, 1835–1914* (London: RIBA Publications, 1971).

4. Dates provided in parentheses indicate the construction period for major projects.

5. D. Arkin, "Perspektivnyi plan Peterburga, 1764–1773," *Arkhitekturnoe nasledstvo*, 1955, no. 7:13–38.

6. N. Leiboshits and V. Piliavskii, "Materialy k istorii planirovki Peterburga v pervoi polovine XIX veka (1800–1840-e gody)," *Arkhitekturnoe nasledstvo*, 1955, no. 7:39–66.

7. N. F. Khomutetskii, *Peterburg-Leningrad* (Leningrad: Lenizdat, 1958), 16.

8. V. A. Kamenskii, *Leningrad: General'nyi plan razvitiia goroda* (Leningrad: Lenizdat, 1972), 16–19, 62–68. These efforts are explained in Marshall Berman, *All That Is Solid Melts into Air: The Experience of Modernity* (New York: Simon and Schuster, 1982), 173–286.

9. Leiboshits and Piliavskii, "Materialy k istorii"; James Bater, *St. Petersburg: Industrialization and Change* (Montreal: McGill-Queens University Press, 1976), 67–69.

10. Iu. A. Egorov, *Ansambli' v gradostroitel'stve SSSR* (Moscow: Aka-

demiia nauk SSSR, 1961). Republished as Iu. A. Egorov, *The Architectural Planning of St. Petersburg,* trans. Eric Dluhosch (Athens: Ohio University Press, 1969).

11. Leiboshits and Piliavskii, "Materialy k istorii," 43.

12. George Heard Hamilton, *The Art and Architecture of Russia* (Baltimore: Penguin, 1975), 227–30. For further description and photographs of the major monuments of Imperial Petersburg, see William C. Brumfield, *Gold in Azure: One Thousand Years of Russian Architecture* (Boston: Godine, 1983).

13. Egorov, *Ansambl' v gradostroitel'stve SSSR,* 81–91; Egorov, *Architectural Planning,* 105–30.

14. *Leningrad: Entsiklopedicheskii spravochnik* (Moscow and Leningrad: Bol'shaia Sovetskaia Entsiklopediia, 1957), 713.

15. Ibid., 184.

16. Egorov, *Ansambl' v gradostroitel'stve SSSR,* 113–26; Egorov, *Architectural Planning,* 183–211.

17. For the importance of these elements in creating an effective public space, see Camillo Sitte, *Der Stadtebau nach seinen kunstlerischen Grundsatzen.* Translated by George R. Collins and Christiane Crasemann Collins under the title *City Planning According to Artistic Principles* in George R. Collins and Christiane Crasemann Collins, *Camillo Sitte: The Birth of Modern City Planning* (New York: Rizzoli, 1986).

18. On the tyranny of symmetry, see Collins and Collins, *Camillo Sitte,* 185–91.

19. A point repeated throughout the work of William H. Whyte. See his *The Social Life of Small Urban Spaces* (Washington, D.C.: Conservation Society, 1980) and his *City: Rediscovering the Center* (New York: Doubleday, 1988).

20. Berman, *All That Is Solid,* 189. The power of spontaneity in urban life is explored, among many places, in Brendan Gill, "Fortunate Accidents," in Cooper-Hewitt Museum, *Urban Open Space* (New York: Rizzoli, 1979), 78.

21. Collins and Collins, *Camillo Sitte,* 146.

22. These four include many critical events of the Decembrist Rebellion of 1825, the Revolution of 1905–6, as well as the February and October revolutions of 1917.

23. For further discussion of the evolving relationship between public and private realms in European urban design of the period, see Michael Dennis, *Court and Garden: From the French Hotel to the City of Modern Architecture* (Cambridge: MIT Press, 1986).

24. Andrei Bely, *Petersburg,* trans. John Cournos (New York: Grove Press, 1959), 57. This transformation is also discussed in Berman, *All That Is Solid,* 249–70.

25. *Entsiklopedicheskii slovar'* (St. Petersburg: Brokgauz'-Efron', 1900), 28:311–19.

26. Bater, *St. Petersburg,* 408.

27. A point frequently made by Soviet commentators who prefer to blame the capital's deterioration on the emergence of capitalism rather than on industrialization. See, for example, Khomutetskii, *Peterburg-Leningrad,* 147–66.

28. *Ocherki istorii Leningrada* (Moscow and Leningrad: Izdatel'stvo AN SSSR, 1957), 3:84–103.

29. Ibid., 2:173–81; 3:104–10.

30. Ibid., 3:894–96.

31. James Bater, "The Legacy of Autocracy: Environmental Quality in St. Petersburg," in R. A. French and F. E. Ian Hamilton, eds., *The Socialist City: Spatial Structure and Urban Policy* (New York: John Wiley & Sons, 1979), 23–28.

32. Hamilton, *Art and Architecture*, 270–75.

33. Ibid, 275–83. Although Fomin's project never left the drawing board, the site was eventually incorporated into a massive residential development. Beginning in the 1940s, local planners began to call for major construction initiatives along the Gulf of Finland. This "movement to the sea" was incorporated into the city's 1966 general plan of development and included recreational areas to the northwest as well as housing minidistricts on the western end of Vasilevskii Island, Decembrist (previously Golodai) Island, and to the southwest. Construction continued into the 1980s, producing kilometer after kilometer of prefabricated housing blocks reminiscent of the worst public housing in the capitalist world. For further discussion of this project, see Blair A. Ruble, *Leningrad: Shaping a Soviet City* (Berkeley: University of California Press, 1990).

34. Karl Schlogel, *Jenseits des Grossen Oktober: Das Laboratorium der moderne Petersburg, 1909–1921* (Berlin: Siedler Verlag, 1988), 36–42; *Ocherki istorii Leningrada*, 3:929–30.

35. Dennis, *Court and Garden*, 1–3.

36. S. Frederick Starr, "The Revival and Schism of Urban Planning in Twentieth Century Russia," in Michael F. Hamm, ed., *The City in Russian History* (Lexington: University of Kentucky Press, 1976), 222–42.

37. M. Lewin, *Russian Peasants and Soviet Power* (Evanston, Ill.: Northwestern University Press, 1968).

38. Kamenskii, *Leningrad*, 33.

39. James Bater, *The Soviet City* (London: Edward Arnold, 1980), 26–27.

40. T. A. Reiner and R. H. Wilson, "Planning and Decision Making in the Soviet City: Rent, Land, and Urban Form," in French and Hamilton, eds., *Socialist City*, 49–71, 57–58.

41. Khomutetskii, *Peterburg-Leningrad*, 182.

42. Bater, *Soviet City*, 26.

43. M. V. Posokhin et al., *Sovetskaia arkhitektura za 50 let* (Moscow: Izdatel'stvo lit. po stroitel'stvu, 1968), 77–79.

44. V. A. Kamenskii and A. I. Naumov, *Leningrad: Gradostroitel'nye problemy razvitiia* (Leningrad: Stroiizdat—Leningradskoe otdelenie, 1977), 126–39; Posokhin et al., *Sovetskaia arkhitektura*, 79–83.

45. Khomutetskii, *Peterburg-Leningrad*, 220; "Nashi zadachi," *Arkhitektura Leningrada*, 1936, no. 1:6–13; L. A. Il'in, "Plan razvitiia Leningrada i ego arkhitektura," *Arkhitektura Leningrada*, 1936, no. 1:18–33; "Slavnoe trekhletie," *Arkhitektura Leningrada*, 1938, no. 4:3–8.

46. *Leningrad: Entsiklopedicheskii spravochnik*, 613–14.

47. Ibid., 506.

48. M. E. Gridman, "Proekty Doma sovetov v Leningrade," *Arkhitektura Leningrada*, 1936, no. 2:8–25.

49. Khomutetskii, *Peterburg-Leningrad*, 216; Gosudarstvennaia inspektsiia po okhrane pamiatnikov, *Pamiatniki arthitektury Leningrada*

(Leningrad: Stroiizdat—Leningradskoe otdelenie, 1975); N. A. Trotskii, "Dom sovetov v Leningrade," *Arkhitektura Leningrada,* 1937, no. 2:8–19; L. V. Rudnev, "Nekotorye zamechaniia ob arkhitekture Doma sovetov," *Arkhitektura Leningrada,* 1937, no. 2:20–33: F. N. Pashchenko, "Stroitel'stvo zdanii administrativnogo naznacheniia v Leningrade," *Arkhitektura Leningrada,* 1939, no. 6:6–19: L. Iu. Gal'pern, "Proekty obshchegorodskogo tsentra v Leningrade," *Arkhitektura Leningrada,* 1940, no. 2:7–25; "Novaia sistema obshchegorodskogo tsentra Leningrada," *Arkhitektura Leningrada,* 1941, no. 1:2–7.

50. Trotskii, "Dom sovetov v Leningrade," 14.

51. Ibid., 15.

52. Ibid.

53. Ibid., 22.

54. N. V. Baranov, "General'nyi plan razvitiia Leningrada," in Arkhitekturno-planirovochnoe upravlenie (Leningrad), *Leningrad* (Leningrad and Moscow: Iskusstvo, 1943), 65–84; Kamenskii and Naumov, *Leningrad,* 126–39.; "O general'nom plane goroda Leningrada," *Arkhitektura Leningrada,* 1939, no. 3:2; N. V. Morozov, "Sotsialisticheskii Leningrad," *Arkhitektura Leningrada,* 1939, no. 3:3–6; and N. V. Baranov, "General'nyi plan razvitiia Leningrada," *Arkhitektura Leningrada,* 1939, no. 3:7–20.

55. Baranov, "General'nyi plan razvitiia Leningrada," in *Leningrad.*

56. Leon Goure, *The Siege of Leningrad: August 1941–January 1944* (New York: McGraw-Hill, 1964), 4–5.

57. Again, these trends are variations on a more general trend toward the private realm in European city building during the past two centuries or so. See Dennis, *Court and Garden,* 101–202.

58. Collins and Collins, *Camillo Sitte,* 198–205.

59. Goure, *The Siege of Leningrad;* Harrison E. Salisbury, *The 900 Days: The Siege of Leningrad* (New York: Harper & Row, 1969); and D. V. Pavlov, *Leningrad 1941: The Blockade,* trans. John C. Adams (Chicago: University of Chicago Press, 1965).

60. Although official Soviet statistics place the number of persons who died from starvation at 632,253, most western observers place the total number of deaths considerably higher. Salisbury, *The 900 Days,* 513–18.

61. Kamenskii, *Leningrad,* 36–38; Posokhin et al., *Sovetskaia arkhitektura,* 150–52.

62. V. I. Piliavskii, *Arkhitektura Leningrada* (Leningrad and Moscow: Gosizdat po stroiiarkh, 1953), 45–46.

63. A. S. Nikol'skii and K. I. Kashin, "Stadion imeni S. M. Kirova," *Arkhitektura i stroitel'stvo Leningrada,* 1950, no. 2:2–16.

64. For further discussion of the later period, see Ruble, *Leningrad.*

65. Thomas Bender, "Metropolitan Life and the Making of Public Culture," in John Hull Mollenkopf, ed., *Power, Culture, and Place: Essays on New York City* (New York: Russell Sage Foundation, 1988), 261–71.

2 RUSSIAN PERCEPTIONS OF AMERICAN ARCHITECTURE, 1870–1917

William C. Brumfield

Iɴ a long digression on architecture in one of the 1873 issues of *Diary of a Writer,* Fedor Dostoevskii made the following sardonic comment on contemporary Petersburg: "And here, at last, is the architecture of the modern, enormous hotel—efficiency, Americanism, hundreds of rooms, an enormous industrial enterprise: right away you see that we too have got railways and have suddenly discovered that we ourselves are efficient people."[1] Here, as in so many other areas, the great writer noted the salient features of an issue that would be much pursued by specialists and professionals, for the terms *enormous* and *efficient* define just the qualities that Russian observers valued in American architecture. In their comments on European architecture of the same period, Russians showed an awareness of nuance and style, and they mentioned the "right" names from the perspective of architectural history. Yet, in the case of America, Russian journals made an isolated reference to Henry Hobson Richardson or Daniel Burnham and John Root but otherwise exhibited an indifference to the specifics of a developing American architectural idiom. What they saw was enormous, colossal, incredible, and efficient.

The Russian architectural press, which conveyed these accounts of American architecture to its Russian audience, was essentially a product of the second half of the nineteenth century; and its development was directly related to the professionalization of Russian architects. The beginnings of cohesion in the profession date from the 1860s, when architects in both St. Petersburg and Moscow realized the need to create an association that would rise above narrow, commercial interests to address problems confronting architects as a group. To be sure, commercialism provided the major financial impetus for a professional organization, as the economic forces of nascent capitalism led to the replacement of the older patronage system of architectural commission with a more competitive, contractual approach to the business of building; but in order to promote the interests of professional development and to regulate the practice of architecture, a form of organization that transcended the individual architect or architectural firm was essential.

The reforms of the 1860s facilitated the economic progress necessary for the expansion of architecture beyond the commissions of the state, the court, and a few wealthy property owners, and they also created the legal conditions for the foundation of private associations. Although certain Petersburg architects had begun to explore the prospect of founding a professional group as early as 1862, the first formal organization was the Moscow Architectural Society, chartered in October 1867.[2] From the outset this organization disseminated new technical information and served as a center for the establishment of standards in building materials and practices. In addition to its advisory function in technical matters, the society initiated a series of open architectural competitions as early as 1868, thus establishing a precedent to be followed in the awarding of major building contracts during the latter half of the century. An ambitious attempt by the society to sponsor a general conference of architects in 1873 failed for bureaucratic reasons, and it was not until 1892 that the First Congress of Russian Architects took place.[3]

In the meantime, architects in the capital obtained imperial approval to found the Petersburg Society of Architects, chartered in October 1870, whose functions paralleled those of the Moscow Architectural Society. At the beginning of 1872, the Petersburg group published the first issue of the journal *Zodchii* (The architect), which appeared monthly and later weekly, through 1917. For forty-five years this authoritative publication not only served as a record of the architectural profession in Russia, but also provided a conduit for information on technical innovations in Western Europe and the United States. It would be difficult to overestimate *Zodchii's* importance in supporting professional solidarity among architects and establishing a platform from which to advance ideas regarding architecture's "mission" in the creation of a new urban environment.[4]

There were other architectural publications in Russia, and a few of them made occasional reference to America; but *Zodchii* remained the major source for information on architecture and civil engineering. The general areas of interest covered in the journal's reports on America included: city planning, construction technology, architectural education, building materials and standards, and the related topic of disasters, particularly fires. Many of the items were taken from American and European architectural journals, as well as from general Russian publications such as *Birzhevye vedomosti* (Stock exchange news), which had obvious reasons of its own to be interested in the progress and economic development represented by new American construction. In addition, *Zodchii* frequently published lectures given at the Petersburg Society of Architects by members who had traveled to the United States, and thus provided firsthand observations of the New World.

From the first year of publication, and every year thereafter, *Zodchii* included news items on the American architectural scene, such as a short comment in 1872 on the new building for the New York City post office.[5] The construction of buildings for public institutions in America's booming cities gained the frequent attention of *Zodchii,* whose editors must have understood that there was a corresponding—if less efficiently met—need for such buildings to serve Russian society following the Great Reforms period. In 1873, for example, there were reports on communal housing for women working in New York's factories;[6] readers of such articles might have been reminded of the housing crisis affecting workers in Russia's large cities. The rapidity of American building methods elicited expressions of wonder that are repeated with ritualistic emphasis throughout the 1872–1917 period. An early burst of enthusiasm appeared in an 1873 article—which was drawn extensively from American publications—on the reconstruction of Chicago after the Great Fire of 1871. The effusive praise reveals much about Russian architectural taste during this period, as well as its fascination with technological innovation:

All of them [Chicago's new "building-palaces"] are built in the latest American style, which represents a mixture of classical, romanesque, gothic, and Renaissance styles; here one can see the widespread use of iron structural components, luxurious entryways even for private houses, balconies on all floors, magnificent roofs and domes encircled with beautiful balustrades. Many of these buildings exceed in luxury and refinement the best buildings of the European capitals and are decorated with statues and colonnades. It is hard to understand how this could have been created in something like a year and a half. Such unusual speed is partially explained by the use of great quantities of iron, including entire facades consisting of a row of iron columns connected by iron beams, and also by wooden construction work (such as at the Palmer Hotel) carried out at night by artificial lighting, and with machines lifting pre-fabricated elements to a height of four stories.[7]

The article's final sentence, echoing similar opinions from *Birzhevye vedomosti,* proclaimed that the new Chicago reflects "the results of moral and material activity such as we have seen nowhere else in the history of the cultural development of mankind."

Indeed, there seems to have been no limit to Russian credulity in the face of American technological ingenuity, as is evident from an item on the "Beach pneumatic tube railroad," intended to carry passengers around the city at a "remarkable speed" far exceeding that of railroads.[8] There was in fact an experimental pneumatic subway opened in 1870 under Broadway Avenue in Manhattan, but its speed and potential for development seem to have been considerably less than remarkable. Pneumatic systems were, however, used for transporting mail in New York by the turn of the century.

Throughout the 1870s, *Zodchii* published a wide variety of articles on developments in American architecture and technology. The subjects ranged from Edison's "Electric telegraph" to engineering topics such as plans for a canal in Nicaragua, bridges in Philadelphia and New York, and American methods for producing ice—a topic of interest even to Russians because the rapid growth of cities required more reliable methods of cold storage for perishable foodstuffs.[9] A direct correlation between Russian and American interests appeared in a favorable review of the Russo-American Rubber Company pavilion at the 1876 Centennial Exhibition in Philadelphia, in which Russians recorded American comments on Russian art.[10] Yet attention remained primarily on American builders, whose accomplishments made St. Petersburg's building boom seem modest.

In general, *Zodchii*'s contributors showed little interest in exploring the principles underlying the new American architecture, but there were rare comments that showed the contributors' perceptions of what the American experience meant for the development of architecture. In an article on the journal *American Architect and Building News*—a frequent source of information for *Zodchii*—the reviewer not only provided a detailed description of the publication, but also commented on what he saw as the pervasive influence of the nineteenth-century French theoretician Etienne Viollet-le-Duc, whose writings played a major role in discussions on the nature of Russian architecture during this period. Particularly noted is Viollet-le-Duc's influence on American "prac-

46

ticality" and on American architects' return to medieval architecture as a source of guidance, not in a literal or historicist sense, but for a new understanding of structural support systems in building.[11]

ARCHITECTURAL TRAVELOGUE: SERGEI KULESHOV'S VIEW OF AMERICA, 1876

The above-mentioned articles, consisting of observations based on material from Russian, European, and American publications, lacked the immediacy of a firsthand report. For the Russian architect who wished to travel, Europe was much closer and its monuments far better known than those in America; yet the interest in American construction could not be denied. The 1876 Philadelphia Centennial Exhibition, with its Russian exhibits, provided an important stimulus to this interest and attracted a number of Russian architects and engineers.[12] Among them was Sergei Kuleshov, whose series of articles in the 1877 issues of *Zodchii* provided the first detailed and informed account of the architectural landscape in major American cities.

Kuleshov's survey begins, predictably, with New York, and it is soon evident that he intends to deal not only with narrow technical questions, but also with the way of life reflected in American cities. Descriptions of building materials and urban planning in New York alternate with reports on features of American domestic life, such as home ice delivery, antitheft devices in apartment buildings, attached "row" houses in city blocks that lack courtyards and have special buildings for parking carriages, and complete domestic water systems. The luxurious houses of New York's "aristocrats of capital" are given their due, as are the city's large hotels; yet the names of the architects never appear.[13]

In the area of technological progress, Kuleshov was most impressed by advances in urban rail transportation, as seen in the widespread use of horse tramways, the development of an elevated railway system, and the plans for building a subway line. Although construction did not begin on New York's first permanent subway until 1900, the underground lines of major railways had stations within the city, and Kuleshov commented on their usefulness. For longer distances, the Grand Central Depot, a French Renaissance building completed in 1871 and replaced in 1913, impressed the Russian visitor as a suitably imposing gateway for his subsequent explorations in America. Other technological advances described in this series include hydraulic elevators, which facilitated the increasingly dense construction in areas such as Wall Street. Kuleshov understood that New York functioned as a metropolis not simply because of its architectural magnificence and technological innovation, but because of the systematic planning and organization of urban services—from public transportation and sewage disposal to such apparently minor amenities as private mailboxes at the post office.

Beyond these technical and practical observations, Kuleshov populates the urban landscape with a series of vignettes on the habits of what is for him a peculiar and fascinating species: *Homo americanus*. Significantly, he registers greatest surprise at American attitudes toward religion, where architecture defined social and economic differences, just as in other areas of American life. Catholic and Episcopal churches were built in the familiar Gothic style, while the churches of most of the Protestant sects adopted a "bold" stylistic resolution devoid of interior decoration and often unidentifiable as a church from the exterior. The transformation of the place of worship into a meeting house is expressive of American democracy, and Kuleshov acknowledges the presence of religious freedom and tolerance in America.

But from the perspective of a Russian Orthodox, Kuleshov is puzzled by the manifestations of such freedom: the rapid turnover in church membership; the boisterous competition among various sects for financial support; and such curious social practices as evening teas for the entertainment of young people, complete with admission charge. His mildly censorious attitude toward the secular concerns of American churches and their desire to "make Money"—a phrase he reproduces in English—is evident in his criticisms of the competitiveness that in other respects forms the base of the stupendous growth of New York during that period. Kuleshov can hardly deny the spectacular effects of the American drive for money and economic development; yet given his own social and cultural instincts, he protests in matters of religion—the one area in which he feels compelled to defend Russian values.

None of this is belabored in Kuleshov's survey, for the writer was concerned primarily with the particulars of his observations. His descriptions of several major buildings in New York are characterized by attention to detail regarding measurements, dates, and materials, as well as by quite specific commentary on how things work, from transportation systems to the glass blocks, or "skylights," on New York sidewalks. He includes a detailed drawing of one of these glass sidewalk grids in his survey. Despite his lack of attention to the work of individual architects, he must have had a very knowledgeable—if unidentified—guide through New York, who clearly responded to the Russian's acuity of vision and curiosity about the idiosyncracies of American life. From New York, Kuleshov boarded the Pennsylvania Railroad for Philadelphia—a journey through what he describes as a boring landscape broken by insignificant towns: Newark, Elizabeth, Trenton, and Princeton. "Along the whole way to Philadelphia the traveler's attention is offered nothing of interest: quite the contrary, his sight is fatigued by the unending view of an entire array of signs with advertisements—primarily from the makers of various spices."[14]

RUSSIAN PERCEPTIONS OF AMERICAN ARCHITECTURE

Philadelphia impressed Kuleshov as a pleasant city, less crowded than New York, and distinguished by its great number of private homes: "Philadelphia is called the 'City of Homes' [in English], i.e., in literal translation, *gorod svoiasi,* in which the majority of families live in their own homes, and, by the way, more comfortably than in other American cities."[15] While commenting on the comfort and reasonable cost of these homes, Kuleshov also notes the monotony characteristic of row houses. The style is described as Franco-American—largely because of the frequent use of the mansard roof with an obligatory bay window, which, he writes, had begun to appear in Russian town houses. He describes the details of construction, from the design of windows to the flat roofs covered with sheets of asbestos, whose properties so intrigued Kuleshov that he devoted an extensive historical sketch to the material's development and uses. Its possibilities as an effective form of building insulation seemed limitless in the latter part of the nineteenth century—a "miracle product," that, despite its fibrous nature, was considered not a hazard to health, but an easily adaptable building material.

In addition to Philadelphia's homey neighborhoods, Kuleshov made note of the city's libraries and schools, including the University of Pennsylvania, which he mistakenly called the oldest institution of higher education in America. As in New York, the competition among Philadelphia's sectarian churches for the allegiance and support of newcomers amazed Kuleshov, who reported that printed invitations to neighborhood places of worship were commonly tossed through open bay windows: "Come, come, come!" The same spirit of boosterism applied to descriptions of Philadelphia's city hall, then under construction. Although he admired the scale of the structure, the Russian observer felt compelled to vent his irritation at the incessant barrage of claims and solicitations that had confronted him since his arrival in New York:

Philadelphians are quite convinced that this tower [over the city hall] will be "the highest in the world" [the emphasis and the English are Kuleshov's]; and this, by the way mistaken, opinion gives them great pleasure. One must note that in general boasting is a peculiarity of Americans, and it appears not just in advertisements claiming any product, any object of American origin—of whatever quality—to be the best in the world, the largest in the world. Such claims frequently appear even in more or less serious publications from across the Atlantic.[16]

Nonetheless, Kuleshov maintained his equanimity in the face of American ebullience, and he continued his travel description with a most favorable report from Washington, D.C., the last city on the tour. Even in the context of Kuleshov's scrupulous attention to factual data on American construction and planning, it is surprising to find a judicious, informed survey of the American system of representational government at the beginning of his article on the nation's capital city. Indeed, one might interpret this extensive account—written for publication in a Russian journal—as indicative of the fitful movement toward political reform within Russia during the latter part of the 1870s. Kuleshov does not editorialize on the subject, and his description can also be viewed as an explanation for the design of the nation's Capitol building—a bicameral legislative system housed in two wings and mediated by a central dome. Nonetheless, these pages form a rare, knowledgeable Russian account of the American legislative forum, and it is worth emphasizing that they appeared in a journal for members of Russia's "pragmatic" intelligentsia.[17]

The rest of Kuleshov's survey of Washington concentrates on various government buildings, which he identifies by their English as well as Russian names and describes in some detail. These include the White House, Department of the Treasury, Department of the Interior, and Department of Agriculture. The survey also describes cultural institutions such as the Corcoran Gallery (the original building, by James Renwick, Jr.), and it devotes particular attention to the Smithsonian Institution Building—the "Castle" on the Mall. After noting the origins of the Institution and identifying James Smithson—the donor of the Smithsonian's original bequest—Kuleshov describes the Castle building: its Romanesque style; red sandstone exterior, with some ten towers of varying height; as well as its interior, complete with exhibit halls, a library, and a chemical laboratory. In summary he notes, "with its multi-faceted and most beneficial work, this institution has acquired wide renown among scholarly societies and institutions of all lands."[18] Kuleshov's concluding comments are dedicated to the city's monuments and the uncertain progress of its most ambitious project: the construction of the Washington Monument.

TECHNOLOGY AND ARCHITECTURE AT THE END OF THE NINETEENTH CENTURY

No subsequent account of American architecture in *Zodchii* demonstrated quite the same breadth of cultural interests that distinguishes Kuleshov's series of articles. Regardless of its geographic or technical limitations, his pioneering account had brought America to life for the readers of *Zodchii,* without slighting the specialized concerns of the architectural profession. It can be argued that architects were particularly receptive to favorable reports on the American republic, by virtue of their interests in economic growth and technical progress. Although architecture had its social and ideological uses in Russian society, Russian architects could praise American buildings and technology without implying political views of either monarchic or radical tint. Indeed, expressions of wonder continued unabated from *Zodchii's* correspondents. An 1879 report on Leadville, a mining town in Colorado, noted that it "sprang up as if by magic" in this "land of wonders." Surely such references would have suggested visions of the rapid exploitation of the rich unsettled regions of Siberia and other parts of Russia. A report on the development of the telephone in America stated: "One can indeed call America the land of application of scientific theories to practice and to life. While we engage in debates over the practicality and future of the telephone, city telephone networks are being created in America."[19]

America was frequently referred to as the standard for comparison in construction and technology, as can be seen, for example, in an article on the efficiency of American housing construction: "Our masons, carpenters, and other craftsmen would be amazed at the speed and daring of the Americans." This highly favorable account took notice of cooperation between New York's housing contractors and municipal authorities in the laying of utility lines and the subsequent paving of streets and sidewalks. Also noted was the reliance on prefabricated, standardized components—for example, window frames and doors—in the design of urban homes,[20] efficiencies that would later become a central part of Soviet housing construction, but on an altogether different scale. Another news item described the opening of New York's Metropolitan Opera House, with the usual hyperbole "enormous."

Beginning in 1882, most of the brief technical news items on American architecture appeared in *Nedelia stroitelia* (Builder's weekly), the newly established weekly supplement to *Zodchii. Nedelia stroitelia* contained excerpts from *Scientific American,* as well as reports from American publications on new buildings, technical innovations, and occasional disasters. Theater fires were noted with particular frequency. In 1885, *Nedelia stroitelia* paraphrased an article from the popular journal *Niva* (Field of grain) on the recent completion of the Washington Monument. Referring to the monument as "colossal," *Nedelia stroitelia* took a very critical view of "an unattractive and crude structure" and said "the monument is striking by the lack of all taste."[21] The tone of this report cannot, it seems, be attributed to anti-American sentiment, but rather to the monument's sharp break with contemporary tastes regarding heavily ornamented memorials—for example, London's Albert Memorial, completed in 1872 by Sir George Gilbert Scott, and the early 1880s entries in the competition for the design of the Church of the Resurrection of the Savior on the Blood in St. Petersburg.

Most of the reports on America in *Zodchii* and *Nedelia stroitelia* dealt with commercial architecture in cities, from Boston and Philadelphia to New Orleans and San Francisco. The centers of attention, however, were Chicago and New York, which represented the most concentrated expression of the American ethos. In the mid-1880s, *Nedelia stroitelia* reported on projects for the building of a New York City subway, elevator construction, the number of houses and firemen in the city, water systems, sanitation, the city's telephone network, and the dedication of the Statue of Liberty. Land prices in New York were "fabulous," but the operative word was "colossal"—as in a "colossal new bridge" between New York and New Jersey, or the "colossal building" for the newspaper *New York World,* which was twenty-six stories, constructed from iron, steel, and brick.[22] Although the reporter had difficulty in describing a building of such un-precedented scale, the Russians had finally discovered the skyscraper; during the next decade, reports on this American form would appear regularly in the Russian architectural press.

Appropriately, the first detailed descriptions of the sky-scraper appeared in articles on Chicago, where preparations for the 1893 Columbian Exposition stimulated an interest in the city unparalleled since the Great Fire of 1871. The ex-position was the subject of extensive reports, such as an anal-ysis of the planning and construction of the site, with statis-tics from the German publication *Deutsche Bauzeitung*. The account mentioned the firm Holabird and Roche, a rare oc-casion in which the Russian press identified American archi-tects.[23] Among other news items on the exposition was an ecstatic report on the project for an all-electric house, de-scribed as a glimpse into the future.[24] A general review of construction in Chicago noted that for six years a new type of structure, based on a skeletal steel frame over a reinforced concrete foundation, had been developed; but the reports were tentative and made no mention of specific architects.[25]

In 1893, the crescendo of attention surrounding the Chi-cago exposition reached a peak. The first issues of *Nedelia stroitelia* contained lead articles describing the pavilions and the frenetic, last-minute preparations in the area between Jackson and Washington parks. In addition to reciting the fair's greatest architectural achievements and its surpassing dimensions, the unsigned correspondent acknowledged the guiding presence of Messrs. John Root—whose death in 1891 was noted—and Daniel Burnham, who served as chief of construction for the exposition.[26] After 1893, there appears to have been no further notice of these two pioneers of the Chicago School in the Russian press. Not all aspects of the fair were viewed so favorably, however. A report on the rapid construction of shoddy hotels in the Jackson Park area commented on the extreme fire hazard existing for those who stayed in these "giant cardboard buildings." One brief item repeated a muckraking claim by the *New York Daily News* that more than one thousand workers had died in constructing the exposition buildings, due to unreliable foundations and scaffolding, and that the Chicago newspapers had engaged in a cover-up of the scandal.[27]

In the midst of this folderol, some observers looked beyond the extravaganza of the exposition to the more solid achieve-ments of the Chicago School. One compact but informative report noted that "giant buildings here bear the strange name 'Sky Scrapers'" and contended that Chicago was particularly "rich in these buildings," despite a growing reluctance to insure them.[28] The nineteen-story Auditorium-Hotel, more commonly known as the Auditorium (1886–90), was described as an example of the speed of construction possible with the new technology. The description included an abundance of statistics concerning the building's cost, its height, its weight, the number of bricks needed for construction, and the length of its water and gas pipes. Yet there is no mention of the style of this spectacular building, nor of the architect, Louis Sullivan. For Russian architectural critics, "style" was to be found in Europe; America was the land of statistics and technology.

AN AMERICAN ARCHITECTURAL EDUCATION

An essential component in the development and application of technology is a well-developed system of technical education. Russia had its own excellent institutes of engineering and architecture—particularly in Moscow and St. Petersburg—that derived much from comparable institutions in Germany and France. But as advances in American construction technology became increasingly evident, the American system of technical education received considerable attention. In 1894, a superficial but prominently displayed series of articles on technical education programs in American universities appeared on the pages of *Nedelia stroitelia*. The first part contained descriptive paragraphs on Harvard, Yale, Cornell, and the University of California at Berkeley, as well as a brief explanation of the American system of land-grant colleges.[29]

The second part provided a much more detailed, analytical view of the technical education program at one of the leading schools in the field, Purdue University, with particular attention to mechanical and electrical engineering laboratories. The unidentified author noted that Purdue's workshops were modeled on Moscow Technical School workshops, which had been displayed at the 1876 Philadelphia exposition. The report concluded with observations regarding the American preference for incorporating the functions of technical institutes within universities and emphasized the high level of aid provided to students by American institutions—again, undoubtedly, in an attempt to spur such developments in Russia. Although they still "lagged behind Europe in the theoretical and abstract sciences," American universities provided an easily accessible technical education with a pronounced emphasis on practicality.[30]

At the beginning of the twentieth century, *Zodchii,* which had absorbed *Nedelia stroitelia* and now appeared weekly, published a more detailed and comprehensive survey of architectural training programs at a number of American universities. Drawn from a lecture by Roman Beker at the Imperial St. Petersburg Society of Architects in 1902, this lengthy series began with two articles on Cornell University, the first describing the university's general history and entrance requirements, and the second more specifically discussing its architectural curriculum.[31] Using material published by Cornell, Beker offered details regarding architectural instruction and observed that priorities at the school had "shifted after the departure of Professor Babcock," who was dean of the school from its inception in 1871 until 1897. Charles Babcock is considered one of the guiding forces in American architectural education, but his emphasis on the need for a thorough grounding in technical matters and principles of construction at the expense of stylistic training had met with criticism, according to Beker. Babcock's approach was to be modified under his successor, Alexander Buel Trowbridge, a student of the Ecole des beaux arts who served as the dean of architecture at Cornell from 1897 to 1902.

Beker's second, and longest, installment focused on Columbia University, with the same mixture of general history and detailed information on its architectural curriculum.[32] Although Beker's series contains little specific information on the deans of the American schools, he deftly caught the nuances of pedagogical debates on such issues as the applicability of the beaux arts model to American architectural training. William Ware, the dean of Columbia's School of Mines from 1881–1903, received his training from the earliest American students of the Ecole des beaux arts and had established the first formal university program in architecture at the Massachusetts Institute of Technology (MIT) in 1867.[33] According to Beker, Ware rejected the notion of a school serving as the arbiter of taste, as based on the Parisian model. Yet Beker's very thorough description of the curriculum indicates the influence of beaux arts principles, with strong emphasis on the history of styles and their re-creation through exercises in draftsmanship. Indeed, the more advanced students were expected to re-create historical monuments as an exercise in the understanding of their structure—

a method to which Beker devotes considerable attention. He added that Columbia's specialization in architectural history was greatly facilitated by the resources of the architectural collection at the Avery Memorial Library. Nonetheless, Ware's ambivalent attitude toward the Ecole des beaux arts dissatisfied supporters such as Charles McKim, and he left the deanship in 1903.

Beker's final article surveyed other prominent American architectural programs, primarily those of Harvard and MIT, each of which received a summary of some two pages. The concluding pages gave brief mention of nine additional universities and institutes with architectural training programs, such as the University of Pennsylvania, Syracuse University, Case Institute of Technology, Armor Institute in Chicago, University of Illinois, Ohio State University, and Tulane University.[34] Making intelligent use of information provided by American sources, Beker conveyed a balanced account of the educational system that underlay the explosive growth in American construction and construction technology. His audience at the Petersburg Society of Architects undoubtedly included pedagogues who were confronted with the perennial problem of educational reform in Russia; and although there is no evidence that American universities served as specific models for change in the Russian system, Beker's articles provide further evidence of the extent of Russian interest in the United States and the degree to which the United States served as a standard for Russian growth and development in this area.

Russian journals contained extensive commentary surrounding the competition for the design of the main buildings at the University of California at Berkeley. Funded by a lavish bequest from Phoebe A. Hearst, the project was one of the major architectural commissions at the turn of the century; and from 1898 to 1900 *Zodchii* devoted several items both to the competition and to the apparently limitless wealth of California—a "separate country," according to one writer. An article in 1900 noted that all eleven finalists had received their education at the Ecole des beaux arts—a tribute to the institution and its pervasive influence throughout Europe and America.[35]

AMERICAN PRAGMATISM AND THE NEW URBAN ENVIRONMENT

But however significant the role played by the French school in American design, Russian observers were more interested in the practical results of American technical developments. In 1895, Viktor Evald—the editor of *Zodchii* and one of the most frequent commentators on American civil engineering—provided an account of skyscraper construction in New York and Chicago, with particular attention to methods of foundation support for the steel frames. Impressed by the size and technology of such large structures, Evald took a dim view of their aesthetic qualities and predicted that they would create an urban environment in which "some of the main streets will be enclosed between two rows of tall, gloomy cubes, with small, separate windows in which the sun never peers. Such streets will resemble narrow canals or streams, flowing at the base of deep ravines."[36] This poetic image was followed by the observation that American skyscrapers were intended for use between eight and five, after which time the central areas of American cities became depopulated.

Subsequently, Evald wrote a book entitled *Structural Characteristics of Buildings in North America,* and in 1899, he continued his analysis of the American skyscraper with an extensive report on a fire at the sixteen-story Home Life Insurance Company building on Broadway Avenue, constructed in 1893. His observations regarding the still-far-from-ideal methods of fire prevention in tall buildings were based, in large part, on data from the German publication *Thonindustrie-Zeitung,* which represented the producers of fire-retardant ceramic shields. The article concludes with a humorous touch:

Let us remark in conclusion that because of a translation mistake, several of our Russian newspapers described this event [the fire] as deliberately arranged to test the efficiency of fire brigades and the safety of such structures. Such is the strength of habit: to ascribe to Americans the most incredibly original escapades.[37]

By the beginning of the century, reports on skyscrapers and fires in American cities appeared in roughly equal measure. In 1903, *Zodchii* published a technical review of recent progress in the area of skyscraper construction, with special attention to new methods of insulating the steel frame from the effects of intense heat (many of these advances were introduced after the Pittsburgh fire of 1897). Drawing upon books by Joseph Freitag and William Birkmire—prominent American civil engineers specializing in the design of skyscrapers—the writer attributed the extraordinary increase in tall buildings in America to three basic developments: the cheap and efficient production of high-quality rolled steel; the production of new types of fire-resistant coating for steel frames; and the introduction of rapid elevators.[38]

Fire had, of course, been an enemy of Russian cities from time immemorial; yet there was a specific interest in the spectacular effects of fire on the new American urban environment, even though the lessons to be learned from these conflagrations had limited applications in Russia. The 1904 issues of *Zodchii* contained several items on this subject, among which was a report on the devastating Iroquois Theater fire, in which some four hundred died, and a survey of measures for fire safety in other major Chicago theaters, including the Auditorium.[39] A subsequent article described methods of fire prevention developed by the firm Adler and Sullivan.[40] The culmination of this inflammatory obsession appeared in the journal's extensive coverage of the great Baltimore fire of February 1904. Based on reports in the *New York Herald*, *Zodchii*'s first article provided a general description of the disaster and its effect on the city.[41] The second article took a more technical approach, examining the conditions of large structures after the fire. The conclusion, bolstered by information from the German publication *Stahl und Eisen*, discussed the remarkable progress in protecting steel frames from fire damage.[42]

By the end of 1904, the "Great American Disaster" theme seems to have been exhausted, with the notable exception of the widespread coverage of the San Francisco earthquake throughout the Russian press. One of the three articles in *Zodchii* on the earthquake, entitled "American Energy," emphasized the extraordinary speed with which resources were applied to reconstructing the city, and concluded: "If you compare this colossal vital energy and strength with what we have done and are doing to revive Syzran, which suffered no less than San Francisco, then the picture is very disheartening."[43] Similar remarks on American resilience had appeared in a report on the Baltimore fire, and in each case there seems to be a contrast—implicit or explicit—with Russian responses to such catastrophes.

In addition to these extensive reports on major topics of interest, *Zodchii* continued to print numerous smaller items on the American scene, as evident in a sampling of *Zodchii*'s 1905 bulletins, including articles on the construction of the Hotel Bellevue in Philadelphia; a concrete dam near Ithaca, New York; compensation for American architects; and the endowment of the University of Chicago by John D. Rockefeller. Of considerably greater length was a series of articles by the Russian architect Aleksandr Dmitriev based on his tour of the United States—the first such report since the one by Sergei Kuleshov almost thirty years earlier.

Unlike Kuleshov, Dmitriev was an architect of considerable distinction, and a number of buildings that he designed are still well preserved in Leningrad.[44] This did not, however, make him a more astute observer of American architecture, and his articles appear disjointed in comparison with the series by Kuleshov. In his defense it must be noted that Dmitriev covered more territory—a function of improvements in the American railroad network since 1877—and Dmitriev admitted that his account only skimmed the surface of a vast topic. Nonetheless, his tour from New York to Philadelphia; Washington, D.C.; St. Louis; Yellowstone Park; Chicago; Niagara Falls; and Boston does not convey cogent impressions of any of these locales.[45] In addition, he quite openly considered the centers of America's major cities to be aesthetic disasters, despite the fact that his stated purpose in visiting the United States was to study new applications for iron and steel used for construction. His own work was quite conservative in terms of its style and technical approach. From the beginning of his series of articles, he declared his preference for American suburbs, such as Cambridge, Massachusetts, where churches, museums, homes, and similar buildings could be seen, without the clutter of skyscrapers.

Dmitriev's report has its piquant moments, for example, in his marvelling description of Coney Island, including an exhibit hall with dioramas of the Battle of Santiago (1898) and other great moments from American history. At the same time, Dmitriev was appalled by the proliferation of billboards and signs. His brief but favorable view of Washington, D.C., includes a description of a Romanesque-style house designed by Henry Hobson Richardson, whose work he admired without attempting to place it within the framework of modern American architecture. In contrast to the sedate impression of Washington, St. Louis and its 1904 International Exhibition were portrayed in sharply critical tones. No mention was made of the significant Viennese presence at this event—represented by Josef Hoffmann, Joseph Olbrich, and Gustav Klimt—yet Dmitriev allotted considerable space to ridiculing the exhibit "Journey by Train through Siberia"—a crude attraction that attested to American interest in the Trans-Siberian Railway.

After the pleasures of Yellowstone, Chicago seemed to

Dmitriev overwhelming and distasteful: "By its wealth, as by its filth, Chicago can easily compete with St. Louis. In general, slovenliness must be considered typical for North American commercial and industrial cities."[46] Nonetheless, he praised the Chicago suburb of Evanston, Illinois, and extolled the Arthur Orr house in that city for its comfort and pleasing design. Similar sentiments—that architecture was the expression of tranquillity and wealth—were applied to his description of Boston, which interested him less than Cambridge and its university. On the Harvard campus, Richardson was again lauded for his design of Sever Hall and Austin Hall, both of which were illustrated in photographs, as were a number of other mansions and buildings that Dmitriev admired during the tour. Almost all of them were built of natural stone in the Romanesque style.

Dmitriev's concluding essay is both amusing and indicative of an ambivalence toward America that was typical of European travelers. Upon returning through Italy, he noted: "After the uniformity of American towns, Naples—despite its picturesque filth—seems remarkably attractive." It is not clear why he should distinguish between the filth of St. Louis and that of Naples, but one can sense a fatigue both with the "new" in American culture and with the concomitant rejection of the past—above all in its major cities. Nonetheless, he recognized America's technological superiority—a merit he seemed to value least: "From an engineering point of view, America is the most interesting country in the world."[47] In addition, Dmitriev pointedly commented on the freedom with which he was allowed to view and examine whatever he chose, even including government buildings. This latter observation is italicized in the text and provides another oblique reference to the political situation in Russia. It should be noted that Dmitriev's series of articles was based on a lecture he gave before the Petersburg Society of Architects on January 18, 1905—nine days after Bloody Sunday, the fateful workers' demonstration in St. Petersburg. *Zodchii,* for its part, studiously avoided mention of revolutionary disturbances throughout the 1905–7 period.

VISIONS OF THE SKYSCRAPER

For most of its final decade of publication, *Zodchii* reported with regularity on new developments concerning American skyscrapers. Articles appeared on the Singer Building in 1906, on the Metropolitan Life in 1907, and on buildings by Francis Kimball in 1908. There were also reports on the completion of other major structures, such as New York's Penn Station and the New York Public Library. A brief notice in 1908 commented on the "gigantomania" of Ernest Flagg, probably the most active builder of skyscrapers in New York: Flagg "dreams of constructing a building as high as one thousand feet.... Even the Yankees have had second thoughts about this. There are reasonable people thinking of raising the question of a law to set limits on the flights of artists beyond the clouds."[48] Yet after 1908, for no clear reason, the number of articles on America underwent a drastic, if temporary, decline. In 1909, the only item on America dealt with air pollution in Chicago; in 1910, there was a single report on a new bridge in Philadelphia; and in 1911, R. Bernhard reviewed R. Vogel's book *Das amerikanische Haus,* reflecting a growing curiosity about the American design of the detached house and its suitability as a model for suburban development around Moscow.

The reappearance of articles on American architecture and technology in *Zodchii* was due, in large measure, to the Sixth International Congress on Materials Testing, held at New York's Engineering Societies Building in 1912. Given the standards of the time, it is noteworthy that the journal's correspondent was a woman, Maria Koroleva, about whom regrettably little is known. Her dispatches provide detailed and highly technical accounts of the proceedings, as well as an analysis of the construction of New York's Woolworth Building by Cass Gilbert.[49] To Russian observers, the Woolworth Building represented an extreme example of the American mania for the office tower—a mania that went beyond the limits of economic feasibility, according to the writer of an article on the building, who also noted that its primary function was to serve as a trademark for the Woolworth firms.[50] In a series of postcards entitled "Moscow in the Future," dating from 1913, visionaries in Russia were producing fanciful sketches of a "new Moscow," which bore a distinct resemblance to midtown Manhattan.[51] Indeed, the first tentative steps in this direction had already been taken with the completion of Ivan Rerberg's modest tower for the Northern Insurance Company in central Moscow in 1911.[52]

The increasingly specific technical descriptions of the engineering involved in the construction of skyscrapers and their skeletal steel frames indicate that Russian builders were prepared to undertake such projects. World War I and subsequent events, however, postponed the large-scale application of this technology until the late 1940s. The most significant statement of this convergence between American and Russian goals in civil engineering appeared in Nikolai Lakhtin's two-part survey of the latest techniques for the use of steel and reinforced concrete in New York's skyscrapers.[53] For Lakhtin, Russia's economic future clearly pointed toward the American model in urban architecture:

Industry, trade, and technology are developing, prices for land parcels are growing, telephones and other communications cannot always satisfy demand; in short, circumstances analogous to those in America are gradually arising in our urban centers. These circumstances make it necessary to construct tall buildings, which must be erected on a steel frame.[54]

With this imperative in mind, Lakhtin analyzed the tall building from foundation to wind braces and made detailed drawings of key points in the steel column and girder structure. The same message, regarding the convergence of Russian and American architectural conditions, was propagated at the Fifth Congress of Russian Architects in 1913 by Lakhtin and Edmond Perrimond, both of whom had recently attended conferences in America and returned to Russia convinced of the relevance of the new American architecture.[55] In a separate article, Perrimond described developments in cold storage, sanitation, and water systems, and in steel construction during a visit to the Third International Refrigeration Congress, held in Chicago in 1913.[56] Despite his admiration for such technology, Perrimond was critical of the unhygienic conditions he found in the United States—one wonders in comparison to what.

With the onset of war, visions of growth, progress, and technical development receded, and with them the possibilities of an American-style construction boom in Russia. These visions were undoubtedly unrealistic or premature; Lakhtin once went so far as to compare the subsoil of St. Petersburg with that of New York to assess whether it could support tall buildings. During the war years, references to America dwindled, with the exception of a series of detailed articles written in 1916 by Roman Beker on small community library buildings in America. Beker presented a highly favorable view of these structures because of their design, and also because they seemed to express the democratic belief in education for the people.[57] In 1917, America's entry into the war on the side of the Entente produced renewed interest in the United States; but at the end of 1917, *Zodchii* ceased publication. In a wholly unintended irony, the last article published in the journal bore the title "American Engineers and the War."[58]

AMERICAN ARCHITECTURE AS CULTURAL MODEL

Although *Zodchii* was considered the most important publication in its field, it was by no means the sole source of information in Russia on American architecture. Lay publications such as *Birzhevye vedomosti* brought unique perspectives to American technology and construction; and at the beginning of the century, new architectural journals such as *Stroitel* (Builder)—not to be confused with *Nedelia stroitelia*—and *Arkhitekturniye motivy* (Architectural motifs) also provided reports on developments in America. Furthermore, advertisements for American products, from Otis elevators to various plumbing systems, appeared in lavishly illustrated Russian architectural annuals. In 1906, for example, St. Petersburg's *Annual of the Society of Architect-Artists* contained an advertisement proclaiming the virtues of a "patented American water-supply system" for private homes. Above the text was an illustration captioned "the Kewanee system in operation," showing a neighborhood home owner watering the grounds of his half-timbered frame house, with a septic system and pumping equipment drawn in cutaway.[59] It seems quite fantastic that in 1906—a year of social crisis and widespread violence—Russian architects could imagine building for a population of middle-class suburban home owners.

Indeed, an element of fantasy reigns over many Russian perceptions of American architecture, even those expressed in the pages of solid professional journals—not to mention the more imaginative, if less reliable, passages from literary works such as Maksim Gorkii's *City of the Yellow Devil* (1906). This air of unreality must be attributed in part to the different levels of development between Russia and America at the time, and to the great physical distance separating the two countries. For all of these limitations, there is evidence to suggest that the extensive Russian reporting on American architecture established a receptivity to technology that would continue—and in some respects increase—after the revolution, despite considerable barriers to exchanges of information.[60]

Beyond the specific function of America as a model in civil

engineering and architectural design, there is the broader issue of cultural perception, which *Zodchii* was uniquely qualified to convey. Although technical concerns are of obvious importance to members of the architectural profession, architecture—as an art and a building technology—also participates in the social and cultural values of the environment it shapes. In this respect, Russian reports and articles on American architecture reveal a continual measuring. America is seen as the ultimate standard, regardless of Russia's more immediate relation to Europe. Paradoxically, this taking of measure reflects, on a deeper level, a type of nationalism that seeks a model commensurate with its own aspirations. Only America, with its continental sweep and boundless energy, provided a comparable scale for the challenges confronting Russian builders.

No other form of endeavor in Russia expressed this relation to America as clearly as architecture, with its emphasis on both the pragmatic and the cultural. Whatever suspicions Russian thinkers such as Dostoevskii might harbor toward American culture, the material from *Zodchii* suggests that the two countries have often perceived in each other a set of values and characteristics that are tacitly admired and accepted as one's own. Hence the willingness of Russian observers to repeat the terms of American boosterism—*colossal, enormous,* and *fast*—even while offering skeptical comments. One suspects that these are the terms that have appealed to the Russians' own sense of destiny—terms that, despite immeasurable social and cultural differences, indicate in the broadest sense the presence of shared ideals and common standards.

NOTES

1. Fedor M. Dostoevskii, *Polnoe sobranie sochinenii v tridtsati tomakh* (Leningrad: Nauka, 1980), 21:106.
2. For a history of the foundation of the Moscow Architectural Society, see Iu. S. Iaralov, ed., *100 let obshchestvennykh arkhitekturnykh organizatsii v SSSR, 1867–1967* (Moscow: Soiuz arkhitektorov, 1967), 6–11.
3. Iaralov, ed., *100 let obshchestvennykh arkhitekturnykh organizatsii*, 12.
4. The complicated publishing history of *Zodchii* and its supplement *Nedelia stroitelia* is presented in Iaralov, ed., *100 let obshchestvennykh arkhitekturnykh organizatsii*, 103–4.
5. *Zodchii*, 1872, no. 3:46.

6. *Zodchii*, 1873, no. 9:110, based on material taken from *Birzhevye vedomosti*.

7. *Zodchii*, 1873, no. 9:107–8.

8. *Zodchii*, 1873, no. 7–8:94.

9. See *Zodchii*, 1876, no. 7:85, based on material from *American Architect and Building News*.

10. *Zodchii*, 1876, no. 11–12:120.

11. *Zodchii*, 1877, no. 3:29–30.

12. A small group of professors and students from Moscow's Higher Technical School visited the United States in connection with the school's exhibit at the Philadelphia fair. The three students included Vladimir Shukhov, who became one of Russia's most distinguished civil engineers. For a discussion of his stay in the United States and its relation to his work, see G. M. Kovelman, *Tvorchestvo pochetnogo akademika inzhenera Vladimira Grigorevicha Shukhova* (Moscow: Stroiizdat, 1961), 16–19.

13. "Eskizy amerikanskoi arkhitektury i tekhniki," *Zodchii*, 1877, no. 4:32–34, and no. 5–6:48–56.

14. *Zodchii*, 1877, no. 11–12:100.

15. *Zodchii*, 1877, no. 11–12:101.

16. *Zodchii*, 1878, no. 1:1.

17. *Zodchii*, 1878, no. 7:73–76.

18. *Zodchii*, 1878, no. 7:78.

19. *Zodchii*, 1880, no. 3–4:33.

20. *Zodchii*, 1881, no. 6:49–50.

21. *Nedelia stroitelia*, 1885, no. 15:3.

22. *Nedelia stroitelia*, 1891, no. 3–4:20.

23. *Nedelia stroitelia*, 1891, no. 39–40:385–86.

24. *Nedelia stroitelia*, 1891, no. 26:288.

25. *Nedelia stroitelia*, 1892, no. 46:313.

26. *Nedelia stroitelia*, 1893, no. 1:2–3, and no. 3:10–11.

27. *Nedelia stroitelia*, 1893, no. 21:102.

28. *Nedelia stroitelia*, 1893, no. 14:62.

29. *Nedelia stroitelia*, 1894, no. 36:181–82.

30. *Nedelia stroitelia*, 1894, no. 37:187–88.

31. At the beginning of his article, Beker notes that many of the publications from which he drew his information were provided by Glenn Brown at the office of the American Society of Architects (the American Institute of Architects) in Washington.

32. *Zodchii*, 1902, no. 38:431–38. This article includes student sketches.

33. See entry on William Robert Ware in Adolf Placzek, ed., *Macmillan Encyclopedia of Architects* (New York: Macmillan, 1982), 4:373–74.

34. *Zodchii*, 1902, no. 50:572–77.

35. *Zodchii*, 1900, no. 4:37–38.

36. *Nedelia stroitelia*, 1895, no. 29:155; the article is entitled "Sky Cities."

37. *Nedelia stroitelia*, 1899, no. 8:58–59.

38. *Zodchii*, 1903, no. 51:605–8.

39. *Zodchii*, 1904, no. 8:86–89, and no. 11:137–38, with material from *Deutsche Bauzeitung*.

40. *Zodchii*, 1904, no. 17:207–8.

41. *Zodchii*, 1904, no. 26:303.

42. *Zodchii*, 1904, no. 39:431–35, with numerous photographs of tall buildings standing among the ruins.

43. *Zodchii,* 1906, no. 37:357–58.

44. For a concise survey of Dmitriev's work, see B. Kirikov, "Arkhitektor A. I. Dmitriev," *Arkhitektura SSSR,* 1979, no. 2:31–34.

45. *Zodchii,* 1905, no. 30:337–39; no. 31:345–46; no. 35:381–85; and no. 36:395–98.

46. *Zodchii,* 1905, no. 31:346.

47. *Zodchii,* 1905, no. 36:398.

48. *Zodchii,* 1908, no. 40:375.

49. *Zodchii,* 1912, no. 46:455–59; no. 47:467–70; and no. 48:479–81.

50. *Zodchii,* 1912, no. 52:522.

51. See E. I. Kirichenko, *Moskva: Pamiatniki arkhitektury 1830–1910-kh godov* (Moscow: Iskusstvo, 1977), 95–99.

52. The tower has survived very well in contemporary Moscow. See photograph in William C. Brumfield, *Gold in Azure: One Thousand Years of Russian Architecture* (Boston: Godine, 1983), 335.

53. *Zodchii,* 1913, no. 18:203–11, and no. 19:215–21.

54. *Zodchii,* 1913, no. 18:204.

55. Compare to Koroleva's report on papers read at the technology section of the Fifth Congress, *Zodchii,* 1914, no. 3:27.

56. *Zodchii,* 1914, no. 12:140–42.

57. *Zodchii,* 1916, no. 46:412–16, and the three subsequent issues, with floor plans, photographs, and a bibliography.

58. *Zodchii,* 1917, no. 47–52:226–29.

59. *Ezhegodnik obshchestva arkhitektorov-inzhenerov,* 1906, no. 1, advertising supplement:xxxviii.

60. Extensive reports based on personal observations of American architecture are once again appearing in the Russian architectural press. *Stroitel'naia gazeta* recently published an interview with a faculty member at the Leningrad Engineering and Construction Institute, who had visited American construction sites in 1985 and gave a positive account of what he saw. "Bystree—znachit pribylnei" (Faster means more profitable); even the terms are reminiscent of those in *Zodchii. Stroitel'naia gazeta,* March 3, 1987, p. 3.

3 ARCHITECTURAL DESIGN IN MOSCOW, 1890–1917: INNOVATION AND RETROSPECTION

William C. Brumfield

BETWEEN the final decades of the nineteenth century and the beginning of the First World War, the built environment of Russia's major cities—and in particular Moscow and St. Petersburg—underwent a profound transformation whose origins can be traced to the social reforms enacted during the reign of Alexander II (1856–81). With the expanded role of private capital in Russian economic life and the accelerated process of industrialization, the architectural profession developed an infrastructure, from training institutes to architectural societies, that would define and regulate the art of building in a period of unprecedented growth.[1]

Yet despite the rapid assimilation of new construction methods after the 1860s, contemporary Russian architecture lagged considerably behind that of the major industrial powers, in both the scale and the effectiveness with which advanced technologies and new materials were applied.[2] Factory and commercial structures whose design had evolved in Europe since the 1830s were being reinvented in Moscow and St. Petersburg some four decades later. The transition from an architecture concerned primarily with the court and the state bureaucracy to one capable of operating in the competitive environment of urban capitalism demanded innovative measures from a system ill-prepared to support them.

Notwithstanding the pervasive constraints of an anachronistic political system and a backward technological base, Russian architects made impressive progress in meeting the challenge of urbanization, with results that are still much in evidence today in central Moscow and Leningrad. The proliferation of new buildings included shopping arcades (or the "passage"), large enclosed markets, educational institutions, banks and other financial institutions, hospitals, public theaters, exhibit halls, hotels, and city administrative buildings (the result of a limited extension of local governmental authority during the latter part of the century). The intensive construction of railway stations during the 1840s and 1850s continued in Moscow and Petersburg throughout the following decades, as new lines opened and some of the early stations were demolished to make way for grander structures.

As for industrial architecture, relatively little work has appeared on this subject in Russia; but it is clear that the increasing needs of industry—notably, the metalworking factories—encouraged the development of engineering techniques in areas such as the design of large enclosed interiors.[3] In addition to iron columns, which had long been in use, iron and eventually steel beams and girders became essential components in the building of large truss-supported roofs over unobstructed work space. (Similar techniques were applied to railway platform sheds.) Although these advances, as well as the use of reinforced concrete and skeletal frame

Map 2

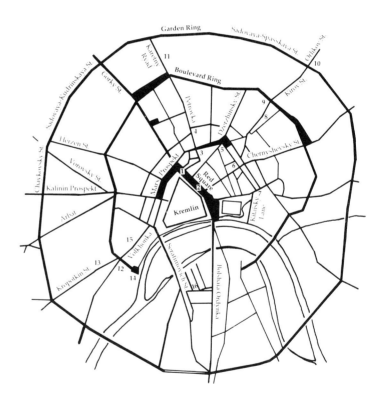

1. Historical Museum
2. Upper Trading Rows
3. Hotel Metropole
4. Muir and Mirrilees department store
5. Moscow Merchants Society building
6. Northern Insurance Company
7. Delovoi Dvor hotel and office building
8. Stroganov School apartments
9. Proskurin apartment house
10. Afremov apartment house
11. Merchants Club
12. Filatov apartment house
13. Isakov apartment house
14. Pertsov apartment house
15. Museum of Fine Arts
16. Tretiakov Gallery

constructions, were considered more the province of engineering than of architecture, the acceptance of new techniques and materials proved aesthetically significant in architecture at the turn of the century.

The most intensive demand for new buildings during the postreform decades occurred in the area of housing, as demanded by the rapid growth in the population of Moscow and Petersburg. Although Petersburg's growth was more noticeable by virtue of its concentrated urban plan, Moscow experienced a comparable increase in population: between the early 1860s and 1897 the city's population more than doubled, from approximately 400,000 to almost 980,000, exclusive of the extensive suburbs the city had acquired by the end of the century. And the majority of this population was poorly housed, if housed at all. Lacking a viable social policy for the construction of subsidized housing, architects had no choice but to build for private interests whose own economic needs accommodated only a small, if growing, segment of the population with disposable income.[4]

In the creation of a new urban environment, Moscow, with its greater availability of land, frequently avoided Petersburg's concentrated development of large city blocks characterized by massively eclectic decorative facades. With an emphasis on the national spirit in the arts during the 1870s and 1880s, projects such as the Historical Museum, by Vladimir Shervud (1874–83; Fig. 25) and the Moscow City Hall or Duma (1890–92; Fig. 26) by Dmitrii Chichagov reproduced elements from sixteenth- and seventeenth-century churches in large secular structures that dominated major spaces in central Moscow.

The culmination of this "pseudo-Russian" style appeared on Moscow's Red Square with the construction of a new building for the Upper Trading Rows (1889–93). Designed by the Petersburg architect Aleksandr Pomerantsev, the Upper Trading Rows can be seen as a turning point in Russian architecture, both because the project represented the apogee of the search for a national style, and because it demanded advanced, functional technology on a scale unprecedented in Russian civil architecture. The basic concept of Pomerantsev's plan derived not only from the "passage," which had been used in Russia since the 1830s, but also from the example of the Milan Galleria. Yet nothing in Russia, or indeed Europe, equaled the size of this complex with some twelve hundred shops for both retail and discount trade.

The appearance of the building, calculated to appeal to a

taste for ostentatious display, represented a gesture of historical consciousness on the part of the merchants who paid for the building (Fig. 27). But to justify the project in financial terms, considerable ingenuity was required to reconcile the iconographic purpose of the heavily encrusted facade with the need for a functioning commercial space in the interior. The general plan consisted of three parallel arcades along the length of the structure (242 meters), connected by three passages across its width. Each arcade contained three levels, with rows of shops fronting the passageway on the first and second levels. Walkways of reinforced concrete (possibly the first use of this technique in Russia) spanned the opposing galleries of shops on the second level, as well as the offices on the third level (Fig. 28). The entire three-story space ascended in a set-back toward the great iron and glass arched skylights extending the length of the passage and providing the main source of illumination for the interior.[5]

25 (facing page) Historical Museum. Red Square, Moscow. 1874–83. Architect: Vladimir Shervud. Photo: William Brumfield.

26 City Hall (Duma). Moscow. 1890–92. Architect: Dmitrii Chichagov. Photo: William Brumfield.

The fact that this enormous edifice functioned is a tribute to the engineering genius of Vladimir Shukhov, who specialized in the design of large metal-frame structures, and to the high level of technical proficiency achieved in Russian construction at the turn of the century. The use of reinforced concrete for the interior walls and vaulting eliminated the need for thick masonry support walls and provided the space for circulation and light. In addition, the complex was serviced by a complete network of basement corridors, beneath which was a subbasement with heating boilers and an electrical generating station.

Despite these impressive resources, the Upper Trading Rows revealed a fundamental disjunction between the insistence on a national style and the rational, functional demands of modern urban architecture. It could be argued that Pomerantsev's design of the facades provided an appropriate complement to the other structures on Red Square, without sacrificing the functional arrangement of the interior. Nonetheless, the draping of a large commercial center with motifs

27 Upper Trading Rows. Red Square, Moscow. 1889–93. Architect: Aleksandr Pomerantsev. Photo: William Brumfield.

of historical reminiscence showed little promise from either an aesthetic or economic point of view. Indeed, many prospective tenants saw little advantage in moving to the small, tightly segmented shops of the new building, which yielded only a very modest return to the investors who had bought five million rubles worth of stock in the Society of Trading Rows. The union between the "national" and the "rational," advocated in late nineteenth-century architectural criticism

28 Upper Trading Rows. Interior. Photo: William Brumfield.

and attempted on a grand scale in the Upper Trading Rows, revealed a fundamental disjunction between accepted notions of style—based on the decorative articulation of a masonry facade—and the need for a more functional tectonic system in commercial architecture.

The appearance in Russian architecture of a "new style," or style moderne (both terms were used in the professional press at the beginning of the century), attempted to readjust the relation between decoration and structural design. In this task architects relied heavily on the precedent of European movements such as art nouveau and the Vienna Secession. Reports on the work of Victor Horta, Joseph Maria Olbrich, Otto Wagner, and other contemporary European architects appeared frequently in Russian architectural publications, as did articles on such topics as the vernacular revival in the design of houses in Great Britain. With a rapid, if highly uneven, capitalist economic development in Russia, the possibilities for assimilating new architectural models from abroad led to a movement whose primary characteristics were a free approach to style and the extensive application of construction materials such as ferroconcrete and plate glass. Beyond these few shared traits, the diversity of the style moderne could embrace both the extensive application of decorative arts, and a design rationalism that dispensed with facade decoration almost entirely.

For all the public attention bestowed by the Russian press upon the new architecture at the turn of the century, there is no clear point of origin for the transformation that occurred in Russian architecture at that time. There were no programmatic statements, such as Otto Wagner's *Moderne Architektur,* nor were there buildings such as Joseph Olbrich's Secession House to announce the new style. The speeches delivered at the Third Congress of Russian Architects, held in Petersburg in 1900, made no substantial reference to new developments in architecture, yet the speakers had all but abandoned the debate over the relevance of medieval Russian architecture for the creation of a national style. Indeed, this was the first major conference in which engineering topics clearly predominated over the aesthetic.[6]

The greater attention given to building technology at the turn of the century did not imply that aesthetic issues had been neglected in favor of pragmatism. The frequent references in architectural journals to John Ruskin, William Morris, the English Arts and Crafts movement, and the work of artists associated with the Abramtsevo community demon-

74

strate that aestheticism in both design and architecture en-joyed unprecedented vigor in an era of commercial and industrial expansion.[7] Yet the actual creation of a "new style," the moderne, seems to have filtered into Russian architecture without proclamation or direction. The style moderne, whose realization in Moscow and Petersburg displayed con-siderable differences, assumed and maintained a protean char-acter reflecting its many sources of inspiration, from Vienna to Glasgow.

In view of its diversity of sources and forms, one must conclude that the style moderne is fundamentally eclectic— not in the nineteenth-century sense of the patterned facade or the historicist stylization, but in the inventive combination of structure, material, and decorative motif. For this reason it is difficult to define the initial appearance of the moderne and trace its development in a strict sequence through the work of a select group of architects. Russian architectural practice at this time was more adaptable, with an eye to the striking decorative effect; and the career of every notable proponent of the new style demonstrated an ability to inter-pret it in widely divergent ways—or to discard it when chang-ing tastes dictated a different approach. This phenomenon of change and adaptability was particularly evident in Moscow, where the style moderne achieved its most distinctive expres-sion in a series of buildings ranging from hotels and museums to apartment houses.

★   ★   ★

The transition to the new style and the extent of the change it entailed were first demonstrated on a large scale in Mos-cow's Hotel Metropole, begun at the end of the century. Commissioned by the Petersburg Insurance Society to pro-vide Moscow with a hotel that would meet international standards of design and luxury, the Metropole had a very complicated construction history. Even the winning design of William Walcot was substantially modified—in certain re-spects almost beyond recognition—before work began in 1899. During the five years of construction (which included rebuilding after a severe fire in 1902), other artists and ar-chitects were involved in the project, most notably Lev Kek-ushev, who supervised the construction and added a number of elements of his own.

There are many aspects of the Metropole that serve to classify it as a landmark of the style moderne; although it has elements of horizontal and vertical emphasis, and a large arched form at the center of the main facade, the facade itself contains virtually no reference to the order system (Fig. 29). The new style developed a concept of tectonics in which structural mass could be shaped without reference to illusionistic supporting elements. Texture and material acquired the dominant expressive role, exemplified at the Metropole by the progression from an arcade with stone facing on the ground floor to the upper floors in plaster over brick, with inset windows lacking any decorative frame. The central two stories are contained within two horizontal strips formed by wrought-iron balconies; vertical accents are provided by glass bays in the center and at the corners of the main facade. The patterned brick surface of the uppermost floor completes the contrast of texture and material, in which the decorative arts and structural form are combined.

Paradoxically, this new relation between structure and material at the Metropole enabled the architect to use the facade as a ground upon which other art forms could be mounted, such as the plaster frieze by Nikolai Andreev on the theme

29　Hotel Metropole. Moscow. 1899–1904. Architect: William Walcot. Photo: William Brumfield.

"The Four Seasons" (along the fourth floor), and seven ceramic panels designed by Aleksandr Golovin above the fifth story. Most prominently, the great arch at the center of the main facade contains the ceramic panel "The Princess of Dreams" (from the play by Rostand), designed by Mikhail Vrubel. It is significant that both Vrubel and Golovin had been active in the Abramtsevo community, whose commitment to the arts and crafts revival and to an integrated concept of structure and decoration are so largely displayed at the Metropole.

From the modest experiments of amateurs at Abramtsevo to the unprecedented scale of a "first-class hotel" (as it was labeled in the competition projects), a new aestheticism had asserted its presence in a reinforced-concrete building, financed by an insurance company and demanding the most advanced technical resources. As the first major example of the new style in Moscow, the Metropole also revealed a tension between structure and decoration characteristic of most early examples of the moderne. Whatever the ideal, in practice the attempt to integrate art and structure might lead to a superficial application of decorative motifs associated with art nouveau, or, in the case of the Metropole, a contest between structural clarity and the use of the facade as a surface on which to display the work of artists and sculptors.

The balance between function and decoration was not, however, beyond the reach of a gifted architect with a clearly defined idea of his building's purpose. Such was the case in Viktor Vasnetsov's design for the expansion of the Tretiakov Art Gallery, and it is altogether appropriate that the painter-architect who had contributed so much to the success of the Abramtsevo colony in the final two decades of the nineteenth century should have gained the opportunity to design a building devoted to the first major display of Russian art in Moscow (Fig. 30).

Vasnetsov did not, in fact, build the entire Tretiakov Gallery. Although the details of the construction history are not altogether clear, he was commissioned around 1900 to create a new main entrance and facade for the gallery, which had been in existence as a public museum since 1892, when the merchant Pavel Tretiakov donated his collection to the city of Moscow.[8] The building that housed the collection formed part of an earlier complex of structures, including warehouses as well as the Tretiakov home, whose space was initially expanded in 1873 to accommodate a private art collection. In providing a focal point for the assortment of structures grouped around a central yard, Vasnetsov attached an entrance facade (projecting into the yard) to the long building that held most of the paintings. Work on the facade decoration can be firmly dated to 1903 and was probably completed in 1905.[9]

Vasnetsov's conception of the entrance made use of a simple brick facade, lightly stuccoed and painted, to provide a clear spatial outline, as well as to provide a base for the Russian folk-style decorative bands along the upper part of the facade. The strips include, in descending order, a ceramic frieze in a design resembling fin de siècle symbolist painting, a large inscription (announcing the Tretiakov donation) on a white background in the style of a medieval Russian manuscript, and a decorative brick border. The adaptation of Russian motifs at the entrance to the Tretiakov Gallery differs from that of the "pseudo-Russian" style, with its facades encumbered with a literal reproduction of decorative motifs. For Vasnetsov a solitary window with decorative surround

30   Tretiakov Gallery. Moscow. 1900–1905. Architect: Viktor Vasnetsov. Photo: William Brumfield.

78

fulfills the function of a museum display, a carefully considered reference to an artistic system of the past.

None of these references to the Russian artistic heritage obscures the union of structure and function realized in the entrance, centered beneath the barrel roof, whose contours point downward to a two-story window and to a porch in the style of medieval Muscovy. Above, the museum skylights echo the pointed forms of the porch and a relief sculpture of St. George slaying the dragon (the heraldic symbol of the city of Moscow). Vasnetsov's task was facilitated by the gallery's specifications for overhead lighting, thus eliminating the need for windows that would have interfered with his design of the facade. Yet it is the artist's clarity of vision that endowed the tectonic form with qualities that are both painterly and rational, redolent of Russian art and suited to the function of a modern gallery.

The use of traditional decorative elements within a new architectural aesthetic was pursued still further by Fedor Shekhtel in his rebuilding of the Iaroslavl Railway Station— a project concurrent with Viktor Vasnetsov's work at the Tretiakov Gallery. Shekhtel and Vasnetsov were both in the forefront of a revival of the Russian architectural tradition through an aestheticized, free-style approach known as the "neo-Russian" style (as opposed to the earlier, ponderously literal "pseudo-Russian" manner). In Shekhtel's case, the neo-Russian style can be related to wooden prototypes, such as those that he had used to spectacular effect in designing the Russian pavilions at the 1901 Glasgow Exposition.[10] At the same time, the towers at each corner of the station are modeled on brick fortress and monastery walls that exist in rich profusion in both Moscow and Iaroslavl, key points in this northern railway network that had originally been created by Savva Mamontov. The free interpretation of these forms by Shekhtel was intended to suggest the colorful, asymmetrical image of medieval Russian architecture (Fig. 31).

A report in the first issue of *Zodchii* (The architect) for 1905 made specific reference to the symbolic nature of the recently completed station and its decorative elements:

This railroad, connecting Moscow with the north of Russia, itself determined, as it were, the question of the facade's style; thus a northern Russian character was considered most appropriate for the new reconstruction. The larger part of the facade is faced in gray brick. Under the main tower is a relief portraying Saint George the Dragon-Slayer, the Archangel Michael, and a bear with a poleaxe—the emblems of Moscow, Arkhangelsk, and Yaroslavl. All other decorations are of colored majolica tiles prepared according to designs by Academician F. O. Shekhtel at the Abramtsevo workshop of S. I. Mamontov.[11]

As at the Hotel Metropole, the arts and crafts center of Abramtsevo provided the means for incorporating the applied arts into the aesthetic system of the new architecture. The ceramic tiles referred to above formed a green and brown frieze along the main facade of gray pressed brick, which merged into the massive turrets on either side of the main entrance (Fig. 32). At this central point the decorative possibilities of ceramic, stucco, and iron were explored with attention to both texture and symbolism, as in the gargantuan representation of wild strawberries in ceramic tile on the turrets flanking the entrance.

Fantasy, however, played little part in Shekhtel's com-

31 Iaroslavl Station. Moscow. Architect: Fedor Shekhtel. Photograph from *Zodchii*, 1905.

mercial architecture, which exemplified some of the most advanced functional design in Moscow. After a transitional stage illustrated in the design of the Kuznetsov store (Fig. 33), Shekhtel's construction in 1901 of the building for the Moscow Insurance Society on Old Square (behind the Kitai-gorod wall) represented a shift from the application of Renaissance decoration within a facade dominated by the arch, to an orthogonal, grid framework (Fig. 34).[12] Although the Insurance Society building—more commonly known as "Boiars' Court," after the hotel situated in the building— retains a number of stucco decorative devices familiar from earlier buildings, the rationalism of its design signaled the beginning of the modern era in Moscow's financial district.

32 Iaroslavl Station. Main entrance. 1903. Photo: William Brumfield.

The clearest expression of the new rationalist approach in Shekhtel's work occurred in two buildings constructed toward the end of the decade: the printing works of the newspaper *Utro Rossii* (1907) and the office building of the Moscow Merchants Society (1909). The first of these exemplified the aesthetics of the machine age in a structure designed to house modern printing presses (Fig. 35).[13] The image of modernity acquires added significance because the newspaper belonged to, and served the political goals of, Pavel Riabushinskii, a leading advocate of a coalition to advance the interests of Russian capitalism.

Like Shekhtel's other commercial structures of the period, the office building of the Moscow Merchants' Society on New Square did not involve a particularly advanced construction technology. In size it occupies a position between the much larger Boiars' Court—located down the Kitaigorod wall on Old Square—and buildings such as the *Utro Rossii* printing works. It shares with all of these the extensive application of reinforced concrete (for the construction of floors and structural members of the main facade), combined with load-bearing brick walls and iron columns for interior support. Despite its virtual lack of architectural ornament and the rectangular grid of the facade, the Merchants' Society building demonstrates Shekhtel's interest in the aesthetic properties of building materials, such as the yellow pressed brick of the facade and the sheets of tinted plate glass (Fig.

33   M. S. Kuznetsov building. Moscow. 1899. Architect: Fedor Shekhtel. Photo: William Brumfield.

36). (Although the basic structure is intact, the building has been considerably modified in recent decades.)

In the area of retail trade, the most notable development in the new architecture was Roman Klein's design of a large department store for the firm of Muir and Mirrielees (1906–

34 Moscow Insurance Society building (Boiars' Court). Moscow. 1901. Architect: Fedor Shekhtel. Photo: William Brumfield.

8). Klein's earlier emporium for the wholesale trade at the Middle Trading Rows had attempted to fuse historicism with the serviceable commercial space, as had Pomerantsev in the construction of the adjacent Upper Trading Rows. Slightly over a decade later, the requirements for a modern, unified retail space led to a radically different design. As with the Hotel Metropole, the primary goal lay in creating an "international class" setting that would provide convenience to the customer and at the same time rationalize the operation of retail merchandising from small shops in trading rows to one universal store.

With his design of a reinforced concrete frame to support the structure, the building was probably the first in Moscow to use a system of suspended exterior walls, whose strips of

35 *Utro Rossii* building. Moscow. 1907. Architect: Fedor Shekhtel. Photo: William Brumfield.

plate glass provided natural illumination for the interior (Fig. 37). Klein chose to emphasize the lines of the facade grid, but he retreated from creating an unadorned, modernist structure: like certain of his American contemporaries, he endowed the building with an English gothic decorative overlay that is particularly noticeable along the roof line and on the corner tower. In addition to pinnacles, lancet windows, and crockets, a large rose window dominates one corner of the south facade; yet the gothic elements do not alter in any substantial way the perception of the building's functional grid. Even the ornament itself was based upon the innovative use of materials such as zinc (with an overlay of copper to simulate bronze) and marble aggregate.[14]

★ ★ ★

The most decisive impact of the style moderne on the architecture of Moscow occurred in the construction of housing, where its emphasis on the decorative arts and a more rational arrangement of interior space formed an integral part of the design of both the private house and the apartment building. Indeed, it can be said that in Moscow the large apartment building is essentially a product of the new style, whose standards of efficiency, comfort, and technological progress were suited to accommodate the growth of an increasingly prosperous professional and middle class living in the central area of Moscow. Despite a desperate housing shortage for the lower classes, large parts of the city were still underbuilt; therefore, the construction of large apartment

36 Moscow Merchants' Society Building. Moscow. 1909. Architect: Fedor Shekhtel. Photo: William Brumfield.

complexes made economic sense only if the building design attracted a sufficiently prosperous clientele.

A notably successful example of this trend appeared in N. M. Proskurin's design of two large apartment blocks on Chistoprudnyi Boulevard for the Rossiia Insurance Company (1899–1902). The distinctive style contains elements from the Italian Renaissance (Fig. 38), with a dominant corner tower in imitation of Spasskii Tower, the main entrance to the Kremlin. Le Corbusier was apparently much taken with the design, which represented a self-contained habitation, with

37 Muir and Mirrielees department store. Moscow. 1906–8. Architect: Roman Klein. Photo: William Brumfield.

an attractive open courtyard in the center. Indeed, the primitive services offered by Moscow at the beginning of the century made it essential that such a large project provide its own source of water, heat, and electricity.[15] The substantial investment required for a building and services on this scale was generally available only from insurance companies (as with the Hotel Metropole), and the Rossiia firm had already undertaken another apartment complex the preceding year (1898) on Lubianka Square. Although these two projects show little evidence of the stylistic traits of the moderne, they nonetheless depended on the same economic and social factors essential for the development of the new style.

A more flamboyant use of the plasticity of material occurred in the work of the prominent Moscow architect Lev Kekushev, whose own house (1903) is one of the best examples of the decorative manner of the new style (Fig. 39). His apartment house for Isakov on Prechistenka (Kropotkin) Street (1906) combines the style moderne with a neobaroque use of sculpted figures typical of art nouveau. But apart from the curved mullions of the windows and the great undulating metal cornice, the main expressive element of the design cen-

38   Rossiia Insurance Company apartment buildings. Moscow. 1899–1902. Architect: N. M. Proskurin. *Zodchii*, 1905.

ters on Kekushev's molding of the brick facade (Fig. 40). From the projecting bays at either end to the recessed balcony at the center of the building, the facade is sculpted with a knowledge of the tensile properties of the material that had been so praised as the ideal medium for rational architecture three decades earlier. A similarly fluent approach to material and structure appeared in G. A. Gelrikh's design of the Skopnik apartment building (1908) on Sadovyi-Kudrinskii Street, part of the Garden-Ring Boulevard (Fig. 41).

39 Kekushev house. Moscow. 1903. Architect: Lev Kekushev. Photo: William Brumfield.

Despite the modern disdain for stucco ornamentation, a number of Moscow's apartment buildings for the affluent reached absurd lengths in facade decoration, as is evident from the "castle" built by V. E. Dubovskii for A. T. Filatova on the Arbat (1913–14; Fig. 42). Since the beginning of the decade, Dubovskii had specialized in apartment houses whose pretentiousness commanded high rates, both for himself and for the property owner. In 1909 he had completed another building, with an outlandish molded facade, for the merchant

and rentier Filatov on a prominent site at the head of Ostozhenka Street (Fig. 43). The structure's ornament was so
peculiar that it provoked comment in the *Moscow Weekly:*

Every new year brings Moscow several dozen new monstrously
absurd buildings, which tear into the city streets with a sort of
special abandon peculiar only to Moscow. Where else would you
find something like the new [apartment] house at the beginning of
Ostozhenka?[16]

In the midst of these stylistic effusions, there were apartment complexes whose design reflected the need for functional structures to accommodate the rapidly increasing
demand for living space in the central city. One of the earliest
examples of middle-level housing on a colossal scale in Moscow was L. Shishkovskii's eight-story apartment house for
F. I. Afremov (1904). Located on Sadovyi-Spasskii Street,

40 Isakov apartment
house. Moscow. 1906. Ar-
chitect: Lev Kekushev.
Photograph from *Ezhegod-
nik moskovskogo arkhitektur-
nogo obshchestva* (Annual of
the Moscow Architectural
Society [*EMAO*]), 1910–
11.

42 (facing page) A. T. Filatova apartment house. Moscow. 1913–14. Architect: V. E. Dubovskii. Photo: William Brumfield.

41 Skopnik apartment house. Moscow. 1908. Architect: G. A. Gelrikh. Photo: William Brumfield.

the building resulted from the boom in apartment construction along the Garden Ring, a circular thoroughfare composed of several tree-lined segments. The extension of a tram network in 1904 brought such previously outlying districts within convenient reach of the center, while the larger sites available in areas around the Ring permitted new configurations in apartment blocks, beyond the rectangular slab or the enclosed courtyard. The Afremov building, for example, had perpendicular wings extending from the back facade, thus increasing the amount of space, yet still meeting minimal standards for light and ventilation. The functionalism represented by the Afremov building could, in the hands of a

gifted architect, be combined with a refined use of the decorative arts—as is illustrated by Shekhtel's large apartment complex for the Stroganov School (1903; Fig. 44).

Whatever their stylistic point of reference—Paris, Vienna, or an idiosyncratic variation—all of the apartment dwellings surveyed above show a break with concepts of design prevalent during the 1890s, in either the eclectic or Russian revival style. Yet the possibilities of using traditional motifs in a modern context, demonstrated by Vasnetsov in his design

43 Filatov apartment house. Moscow. 1909. Architect: V. E. Dubovskii. Photo: William Brumfield.

for the entrance to the Tretiakov Gallery, also appeared in the construction of apartment buildings. No one in Moscow proclaimed these possibilities more dramatically than the artist Sergei Maliutin in his design for the apartment house of N. P. Pertsov at Prechistenka Quay (1905–7). Maliutin had already achieved a reputation for his work in the arts and crafts community at Talashkino (the estate of Princess Maria Tenisheva, who also served as patroness of the community). In 1901 he designed the famous *Teremok* at Talashkino, a log structure decorated with fanciful interpretations of Russian folk art and resembling the Russian pavilion designed by Konstanin Korovin and Aleksandr Golovin for the 1900 Paris Exposition. Examples of Maliutin's craftwork were on display at this pavilion.[17]

In his design for the Pertsov building, Maliutin used ceramic panels and other ornamentation based on exaggerated representations of folk art (Fig. 45). The theatricality of Maliutin's sketch for the building—reproduced in the 1907 issue

44 Stroganov School apartment house. Moscow. 1903. Architect: Fedor Shekhtel. Photo: William Brumfield.

of the Annual of the Society of Architect-Artists—masked the basic structure with a panoply of steep roofs, towers, decorated balconies and window surrounds, large ceramic panels, as well as door and window openings of unusual configurations. Although Maliutin intended to reproduce the asymmetry of the medieval *teremok* (a term that includes concepts of "tower" and "chambers"), the extravagance of his free-style design was modified by the architect who constructed the building, Nikolai Zhukov.

A similar collaboration between artist-designer and architect-builder is represented by the "neomedieval" decoration of the apartment house for the Church of the Trinity on the Mire. In his design of the facade, the artist, Sergei Vashkov, made inventive use of patterns from limestone carvings on twelfth-century churches in the area of Vladimir (Fig. 46). Vashkov was also known for his design of church furnishings, and he applied similar crafts techniques to the details of interior space, such as the stairways. The architect of the building, completed around 1909, was P. K. Michini.

Although such colorful, theatrical designs were exceptional, apartment builders in Moscow often seemed infatuated with playful decorative effects—intended, perhaps, to obscure the larger urban monotony. And despite the acceleration of apartment construction during the first decade of the twentieth century, most projects with any claim to architectural distinction remained beyond the reach of the vast majority of the city's population. Advances in building technology, along with a concern for functionalism, comfort, and hygiene, contributed considerably to the development of new housing in Moscow. Yet the innovations cannot be called

45 N. P. Pertsov apartment house. Moscow. 1905–7. Architects: Sergei Maliutin, Nikolai Zhukov. Photo: William Brumfield.

profound in either social or theoretical terms: the economic system that supported the construction of speculative apartment complexes remained untouched by social reform, despite the rise of housing cooperatives and privately subsidized housing such as that of Solodovnikov.

Furthermore, the possibility that an improved technological capability applied in a rational way could lead to new solutions in the design and financing of workers' housing proved premature, although the issue was not ignored in prerevolutionary journals. The apartments located in style

46 Apartment house for the Church of the Trinity on the Mire. Moscow. ca. 1909. Architects: Sergei Vashkov, P. K. Michini. *EMAO*, 1909.

moderne buildings were designed for the prosperous few and contained three or four main rooms placed along the street facade, with the bedrooms and service areas (kitchen, storage, bathroom) situated toward the interior of the building.[18] Apartments of this type had two staircases: the main, or front, entrance and a back service staircase. Improvements in the quality of living space were considerable, yet such apartments formed the exception to the general housing situation. Upon their expropriation following the revolution, when the housing crisis became still more severe, the spacious floor plans were converted into communal apartments, with one family per room.

★　★　★

As the progressive influence of the moderne waned over the course of the first decade of the century, there appeared a renewed interest in retrospective styles, dominated by a neoclassical revival. Although the revival had its most pervasive impact on Petersburg, it also appeared throughout Moscow in every building type described above. However, to distinguish between the retrospective and modernist components in neoclassicism is a complex matter, since the neoclassical revival represented not only a nostalgic reference to the earlier glory of imperial Russia, but also a variation on the rationalist aspect of the style moderne—with neoclassical elements.

Such was particularly the case in the design of large-scale commercial buildings. Although the neoclassical revival provided a model for cultural institutions and other major public edifices, it did not present a ready solution for new administrative and commercial office buildings required by Moscow's rapidly expanding financial center, located in the Kitai-gorod district.[19] In a form of compromise, architects such as Ivan Rerberg applied classical details to asymmetrical structures of modern design, whose scale far exceeded that of Petersburg's neoclassical banking institutions of the same period. In Rerberg's office building for the Northern Insurance Company (1909–11; codesigned by the Petersburg architect Marian Peretiatkovich, with the assistance of Viacheslav Oltarzhevskii), the basic structure was defined by a functional grid of reinforced concrete and large plate glass windows. Classical elements, such as festoons and masks, appear very sparsely on the facade, with the exception of a tower on Ilinka Street and two corner rotundas on the side facing the Kitai-gorod wall (Figs. 47, 48). These domed structures punctuate the labyrinthine plan, consisting of four connected buildings of five stories; and the architect's use of classical detail at such strategic points seems intended to portray the vertical columns of the grid as components in a modernized classical tectonic system.

This system appeared in an even more austerely functional design in the same area: Ivan Kuznetsov's Business Court (Delovoi dvor, 1912–13), a hotel and office complex located on New Square. The initiator of the project was Nikolai Vtorov, one of the most enterprising of Moscow's capitalists and, in the words of a contemporary observer, "the first to break the age-old traditions in favor of a rational and intelligent organization of commercial business."[20] To this end Vtorov located his project just beyond the Kitai-gorod wall and stipulated the most advanced construction design. The plan included an elongated hotel in three attached segments and a trapezoidal office building for wholesale trade—each from five to six stories in height (Fig. 49).

47   Northern Insurance Company building. Moscow. 1909–11. Architects: Ivan Rerberg, Marian Peretiatkovich, Viacheslav Oltarzhevskii. Photo: William Brumfield.

48 Project
sketch for North-
ern Insurance
Company build-
ing. *EMAO*,
1909.

49 Business Court (Delo-
voi dvor) office complex.
Moscow. 1912–13. Archi-
tect: Ivan Kuznetsov.
EOAK, 1913.

98

Kuznetsov, a specialist in ferroconcrete structures, complied with the functional requirements, but he also provided a neoclassical "cover"—no doubt to mitigate the rigorous application of the grid design on the exterior and to designate the main entrances. The corner wedge of the hotel entrance on New Square is marked by the familiar neoclassical rotunda with corinthian columns and dome, whereas the main point of entry to the office block displays a corinthian portico and pediment hovering over the entrance arch (Fig. 50). This irrational window-dressing stands in contrast to the side facades of the building, which are without ornamentation and display the clean lines and sense of proportion characteristic of a new rationalist aesthetic. A more logical integration of tradition and modern functionalism was achieved by S. B. Zalesskii in his design for the department store of the Officers'

50   Business Court office complex. Side view and hotel. *EOAK*, 1913.

Economic Society (1914), whose central atrium supported a great barrel vault of glass, iron, and ferroconcrete (Fig. 51).

The compromise between functionalism and the neoclassical revival, evident in large commercial office buildings, occurred in every other type of building surveyed above. It would be difficult to define a strict sequence leading from the era of the style moderne to the revival of classicism, yet by 1910 Moscow was being refashioned in the ways of neoclassical monumentality. Although Moscow lacked the regularity of plan and the massed facades with classical details present in Petersburg, local architects were able to use a greater openness of urban space to create classically inspired structures at dominant points in the city landscape, such as Roman Klein's Museum of Fine Arts (1897–1912), Ilarion Ivanov-Schitz's building for the Shaniavskii People's Uni-

100

versity (1910–13), and Sergei Solovev's school for the Higher Women's Courses (1910–12). Even the "Iar" Restaurant (ca. 1909), a pleasure palace built by Adolf Erikhson near the fashionable suburban district of Petrovskii Park, displays the fashion for classical Empire-style elements, combined with details derived from the Vienna Secession (Figs. 52, 53).

In the rapidly changing styles of apartment design, there were numerous apartment houses in Moscow that superficially followed the fashion for neoclassical detail; yet the revival rarely achieved coherent expression in the design of such large forms. Among the exceptions are the Shcherbatov apartment house, built in 1912–13 by A. Tamanov on Novinskii Boulevard in a form that resembles a hypertrophied version of a Moscow urban villa from the late Empire period;

51 (facing page) Officers' Economic Society department store. Moscow. 1914. Architect: S. B. Zalesskii. *EMAO*, 1914–16.

52 "Iar" Restaurant. Moscow. ca. 1909. Architect: Adolf Erikhson. *EMAO*, 1910–11.

and the I. E. Kuznetsov apartments on Miasnitskii Street (1910), another massive Empire design from Boris Velikov-skii and A. N. Miliukov, assisted by the future constructivists Viktor and Aleksandr Vesnin.

In the area of monumental public buildings, the revival achieved a greater success by virtue of its obvious precedents in Greek and Roman architecture. Even here, the impact of modernism could be clearly detected, notably in the work of Ilarion Ivanov-Schitz, who had earlier worked in the style moderne, but subsequently turned to elements from the classical tectonic system, which he adapted on a grand scale. His design for the Merchants' Club on Dmitrovka Street (built in 1907–8; now the Komsomol Theater on Chekhov Street) incorporated a recessed ionic portico flanked by square towers that contain classical elements and at the same time suggest

53 "Iar" Restaurant. Interior. *EMAO*, 1910–11.

a resemblance to the Vienna Secession and the work of Otto Wagner (Fig. 54). The modern appearance is even more evident in the interior design with streamlined, abstract decorative shapes that resemble Viennese motifs of the second decade (Wagner, Josef Hoffmann, Adolf Loos), but also anticipate modern design in the West during the 1920s.

The most versatile and productive adherent of the neoclassical revival in Moscow was Roman Klein, whose contributions to the Russian Revival style, as well as to the moderne, have been noted above.[21] Of the approximately sixty buildings completed by Klein in Moscow, the majority follow some variant of classicism—a reflection of his trip to Italy in 1882, a year after his graduation from the classically based curriculum of the Academy of Arts. The most prominent of these buildings was the Museum of Fine Arts, es-

tablished by Professor Ivan Tsvetaev under the auspices of
Moscow University. In 1897 Klein won the design competition sponsored by the Academy of Arts, and over the next
fifteen years, he spent much of his effort on a project that
had more than its share of frustrations. The uncompleted
building was badly damaged by a fire in December 1904; and
between 1906 and 1908, the course of further work was
threatened when a financial depression affected the largess of
Iurii Nechaev-Maltsev, one of the leading manufacturers of
glassware in Russia and the major private donor to the
museum.[22]

Upon completion of the museum in 1912, Klein received
the title "Academician of Architecture" from the Academy
of Arts in recognition of the complexity of the task and the
monumental appearance of the structure. Indeed, its combination of Greek and Roman elements and the luxurious
finish of the interior as well as the granite- and marble-clad
exterior place it on a level comparable to other major museums and public buildings erected in Europe and America

54 Merchants' Club.
Moscow. 1907–8. Archi-
tect: Ilarion Ivanov-Schitz.
Photo: William Brumfield.

during the same period (Figs. 55, 56). The eclectic manner of the design represents an attempt to incorporate various motifs of classical architecture (both Greek and Roman) within the structure of a museum originally intended for the study of ancient and Renaissance art. Thus decoration and function are logically, if somewhat awkwardly, combined; yet the contrast between Klein's monumentality and the vibrant experiment of Vasnetsov's design for the Tretiakov Gallery provides an exemplary view of the stylistic polarities in Russian architecture at the beginning of this century.

The final, and grandest, neoclassical exercise in Moscow's public architecture before the revolution is Ivan Rerberg's design for the Kiev Railway Station, across the Moscow River via Klein's newly rebuilt Borodino Bridge (1912–13). Rerberg, who graduated from Petersburg's Institute of Military Engineering in 1896, served as an assistant to Klein in the construction of the Museum of Fine Arts, and thus was no stranger to the uses of classical elements on a large scale. Work on the station began in 1914; by 1917 the basic structure

55   Museum of Fine Arts. Moscow. 1897–1912. Architect: Roman Klein. Photo: William Brumfield.

was complete, although the final details were not finished until 1920 due to chaotic conditions during the revolution and civil war.

In the design of the main building, Rerberg adhered to a conservative neoclassical manner, with attached ionic columns on the main facade and end blocks containing arched entrances and surmounted with domed rotundas. A clock tower on the right corner provides the visual dominant to the entire ensemble (Fig. 57). In contrast to the neoclassical detail of the station building, the great platform shed, projected and built by Shukhov, represented the epitome of functionalism in the articulation of its iron and glass grid (47 meters in width, 30 in height, and 231 in length).[23] Here, at least, is evidence of a continuity extending through the three decades of modern architecture in prerevolutionary Moscow, from Shukhov's contribution to the design of the Upper Trading Rows, to his soaring arch over the platforms of the city's rail link to the west.

★ ★ ★

56 Museum of Fine Arts. Interior. Photo: William Brumfield.

The preceding examination of stylistic currents in Moscow architecture before 1917 reveals a considerable diversity of approach to architectural design; and if one were to include private houses and churches built during this period, the variety of forms within the style moderne and the neoclassical revival would be still greater. The focus of the present chapter, however, has remained on the larger architectural forms that had a significant impact on the city. Little consensus existed among architects concerning the proper relation between style and structure or the social role of architecture in creating a livable, ordered urban setting. With the support provided by entrepreneurs and public-spirited merchants, Moscow's architects created a remarkable variety of buildings that served both commerce and culture and were at once cosmopolitan and idiosyncratically Russian in design. Yet this environment had very little to offer the masses of impoverished laborers and peasants who poured into the city in search of work and who represented a world apart from the thin stratum of commercial prosperity.

Even the obvious Russian interest in Western technical innovations found only limited application for local architecture in an economy that could not yet accommodate the massive scale of urban construction in Western Europe and America. In this context Russian planners could only dream (as some of them did) of a cityscape dominated by skyscrapers. Thus the short-lived dominance of the style moderne at the beginning of the century quickly yielded to a revival of neoclassicism; but neither movement had a clear sense of purpose, and even in stylistic terms they ultimately merged

57 Kiev Railway Station. Moscow. 1914–20. Architect: Roman Klein. *EMAO*, 1912–13.

into forms of eclectic decoration applied to a modern, functional structure.

As for the legacy of this period for postrevolutionary architecture, it should be noted that a majority of prominent architects during the first two decades of Soviet architecture had built or designed in the neoclassical mode before 1917; yet there is insufficient evidence to claim that postrevolutionary modernism—constructivism in particular—was based in some essential way on neoclassical principles.[24] At the same time, the technical and aesthetic innovations of the "discredited" style moderne were hardly irrelevant to the further development of architecture in Russia. It may seem paradoxical that the final period of Russian capitalism should have provided contemporary Moscow and Leningrad with so much of their functional building stock; but the buildings of this prerevolutionary period, despite their limitations from the perspective of both avant-garde and Stalinist critics, were expertly constructed and have proved more durable than almost anything subsequently built in Moscow.

As is demonstrated in the following chapters of this book, architecture after 1917 existed within fundamentally altered economic and social conditions. The Soviet system itself imparted a far greater ideological focus to concepts of architectural design—including those of a utopian character based on a compelling desire to surpass Western architecture in creating a new social environment. Nonetheless, prerevolutionary modernism, for all of its protean manifestations, not only established an indispensable technical and professional base for the radical experiments that followed in the 1920s, but also created an urban ambience in central Moscow that would be only partially superseded by the totalitarian reconstruction of the city in the 1930s.

NOTES

1. Moscow had the first formal architectural association: the Moscow Architectural Society, chartered in 1867. The Petersburg Society of Architects was founded shortly thereafter, in October 1870. For a survey of the organization and early years of Russian architectural societies, see Iu. S. Iaralov, ed., *100 let obshchestvennykh arkhitekturnykh organizatsii v SSSR, 1867–1967* (Moscow: Soiuz arkhitektorov, 1967), 5–13.

2. For a detailed discussion of developments in Russian construction technology during the nineteenth century, see M. A. Kozlovskaia, "Razvitie nauchno-tekhnicheskoi bazy arkhitektury i stroitel'stva,"

in Iu. S. Lebedev, ed., *Konstruktsii i arkhitekturnaia forma v russkom zodchestve XIX–nachala XX vv.* (Moscow: Stroiizdat, 1977), 12–40.

3. An excellent study of nineteenth-century Russian industrial architecture is contained in A. L. Punin's *Arkhitekturnye pamiatniki Peterburga: vtoraia polovina XIX veka* (Leningrad: Lenizdat, 1981), 63–92.

4. Population figures are taken from Akademiia Nauk SSSR, Institut Istorii, *Istoriia Moskvy* (Moscow: Akademiia Nauk, 1954), vol. 4, *Period promyshlennogo kapitalizma,* 227. The same volume has extensive information on the economic growth of Moscow during the latter part of the nineteenth century. See also Joseph Bradley, *Muzhik and Muscovite: Urbanization in Late Imperial Russia* (Berkeley: University of California Press, 1985), 119–36; and James Bater's chapters, "The Industrialization of Moscow and St. Petersburg" and "Modernization and Municipality: Moscow and St. Petersburg on the Eve of the Great War," in James H. Bater and R. A. French, eds., *Studies in Russian Historical Geography,* vol. 2 (London: Academic Press, 1983).

5. Information on the construction of the Upper Trading Rows is contained in I. P. Mashkov, ed., *Putevoditel' po Moskve* (Moscow: Moscow Architectural Society, 1913). For a description and detailed plan of structure, see also A. I. Komech, et al., eds., *Pamiatniki arkhitektury Moskvy: Kreml', Kitai-gorod, Tsentral'nye ploshchadi,* 2d ed. (Moscow: Iskusstvo, 1983), 404–5.

6. The proceedings of the 1900 congress were published as *Trudy III s"ezda russkikh zodchikh* (Petersburg, 1905). The Artistic Section, which had been the focus of debate in earlier congresses, was represented by only six papers, one of which dealt with the arcane topic of Schopenhauer's views on architecture.

7. The Abramtsevo estate, purchased in 1870 by the industrialist and railroad magnate Savva Mamontov, became a major center for the arts and crafts revival in Russia and had a significant impact on the development of both architecture and the decorative arts during the four decades before 1917. There have been many studies of Mamontov and the Abramtsevo circle, including N. V. Polenova, *Abramtsevo: Vospominaniia* (Moscow: M. and S. Sabashnikov, 1922); M. Kopshitser, *Mamontov* (Moscow: Iskusstvo, 1970); John Bowlt, "Two Russian Maecenases: Savva Mamontov and Princess Tenisheva," *Apollo,* December 1973, 444–53; and William Brumfield, "The Decorative Arts in Russian Architecture: 1900–1907," *The Journal of Decorative and Propaganda Arts* 5 (1987): 12–27.

8. The most authoritative history of the Tretiakov Gallery is D. Ia. Bezrukova, *Tretiakov i istoriia sozdaniia ego galerei* (Moscow, 1970). There are other accounts of the Gallery's founding, including in English: Beverly Kean, *All the Empty Palaces* (New York: Universe Books, 1983), 66–69.

9. Vasnetsov's work on the facade in 1903 is mentioned in the journal *Zodchii,* 1903, no. 36: 427, and photographs of the completed building appeared in architectural publications by 1906.

10. For an account of Shekhtel's work at the Glasgow Exposition, see Catherine Cooke, "Shekhtel in Kelvingrove and Mackintosh on the Petrovka," *Scottish Slavonic Review,* 10 (1988): 177–205. Shekhtel's use of motifs from the Russian north occurred within a context of recreating traditional decorative forms in nineteenth-century exhi-

bition architecture, from the 1872 Moscow Polytechnical Exhibition to the 1896 Nizhnii Novgorod fair. See E. A. Borisova, "Neorusskii stil' v russkoi arkhitekture predrevoliutsionnykh let," in *Iz istorii russkogo iskusstva vtoroi poloviny XIX–nachala XX veka* (Moscow: Nauka, 1978), 63–64.

11.   *Zodchii,* 1905, no. 1: 13–14.

12.   E. I. Kirichenko notes the relation between the commanding presence of the Kitai-gorod wall and the long horizontal lines of Shekhtel's Moscow Insurance building in *Moskva na rubezhe stoletii* (Moscow: Stroiizdat, 1977), 99.

13.   See Rayner Banham, *Theory and Design in the First Machine Age* (Cambridge, Mass.: MIT Press, 1980), 151–52. Russia had nothing comparable to the Werkbund aesthetic in Germany at this time, although certain major industrial structures in Petersburg emulated contemporary German design.

14.   A description of innovative elements in Klein's structural design of this department store is contained in Lebedev, ed., *Konstruktsii i arkhitekturnaia forma,* 155–56.

15.   Elena Volkhovitskaia and Aleksei Tarkhanov give a detailed analysis of the Proskurin design in "Dom 'Rossiia,'" *Dekorativnoe iskusstvo,* 1986, no. 7: 34–38.

16.   Quoted in Iurii Fedosiuk, *Moskva v kol'tse sadovykh* (Moscow: Moskovskii rabochii, 1983), 79.

17.   Maliutin is the subject of a brief article by Sergei Diagilev: "Neskol'ko slov o S. V. Maliutine," in *Mir Iskusstva,* 1903, no. 4: 173–75. The article is accompanied by an excellent series of photographs of Maliutin's work, primarily at Talashkino.

18.   Vladimir Kirillov provides a detailed analysis of the typical arrangement of apartment space in the fashionable buildings of the period in *Arkhitektura russkogo moderna* (Moscow: Moscow State University, 1979), 90–93.

19.   A survey of new construction in the Kitai-gorod district and its implications for Moscow's future as a financial center appeared in the unsigned article "Novaia Moskva," *Moskovskii arkhitekturnyi mir,* 1914, no. 3: 61–67.

20.   Pavel Buryshkin, *Moskva kupecheskaia* (New York: Chekhov Publishing House, 1954), 198. For a discussion of the technical aspects of the Delovoi dvor structure (a combination of brick walls and reinforced concrete), see Lebedev, ed., *Konstruktsii i arkhitekturnaia forma,* 139–42.

21.   L. M. Smirnov gives a lucid survey of Klein's work in Iu. S. Iaralov and S. M. Zemtsov, eds., *Zodchie Moskvy XV–XIX vv.* (Moscow: Moskovskii rabochii, 1981), 288–300.

22.   Now named in honor of the poet Aleksandr Pushkin, the museum is the subject of an exhaustive two-volume study based on Klein's correspondence with Tsvetaev: *Gosudarstvennyi muzei izobrazitel'nykh iskusstv im. A. S. Pushkina: Istoriia sozdaniia muzeia v perepiske professora I. V. Tsvetaeva s arkhitektorom R. I. Kleinom i drugikh dokumentakh (1898–1912)* (Moscow: Pushkin Museum of Art, 1977).

23.   See M. I. Astaf'eva-Dlugach and Iu. P. Volshok, eds., *Zodchie Moskvy: XX vek* (Moscow: Moskovskii rabochii, 1988), 65–66.

24.   For a discussion of the dominance of the neoclassical revival during

the years immediately preceding 1917, its coexistence with a rationalist approach to design, and its complex relation to the further development of Soviet architecture in the 1920s, see Selim Omarovich Khan-Magomedov, *Aleksandr Vesnin and Russian Constructivism* (New York: Rizzoli, 1986), 15, 34–35. It should be noted that the neoclassical revival proved remarkably adaptable to the heroic enthusiasm of the early period of Soviet power, when architects such as Ivan Fomin, Andrei Belogrud, and Vladimir Shchuko—all of whom had worked in Petersburg—produced numerous designs for public buildings in the so-called Red doric or proletarian classical manner. Such projects bear little relation to the more traditional use of neoclassical elements in Soviet architecture of the 1930s. See also William C. Brumfield, "Anti-Modernism and the Neoclassical Revival in Russian Architecture, 1906–1916," *Journal of the Society of Architectural Historians* 48 (1989): 371–86.

4 MOSCOW'S REVOLUTIONARY ARCHITECTURE AND ITS AFTERMATH: A CRITICAL GUIDE

Blair A. Ruble

Russia, where nothing was known in the way of modern architecture under Czarist rule, seems to have received an enormous impetus in that direction under the Soviet regime. It is becoming thoroughly Americanized, or rather, it is making an attempt at it without however concerning itself with the absurd appendages of American culture.

Bruno Taut, *Modern Architecture*

THE Bolsheviks came to power without coherent urban policies but with an ill-defined sense that existing conditions had to be changed. In February 1918 the new Soviet government nationalized land, and eight months later it abolished private property in cities. These moves elevated the state to the status of single client for large-scale construction and planning efforts—a condition that, more than any other single factor, may explain the absence of diversity that has intensified the oppressive character of much of Soviet architecture.

During the 1920s, Soviet architects engaged in extensive theoretical debates, and factional disputes obscured coherent positions on nearly every urban and architectural issue.[1] Throughout most of the decade, the search for new forms of socialist urban settlement involved competing groups whose origins lay in prewar Europe and Russia. According to the Western viewpoint, these debates narrowed to a dispute between those theorists who demanded the urbanization of rural areas into nodal points, such as Leonid Sabsovich, and their counterparts who proposed the dispersal of cities along continuous linear communities adjacent to transportation and power corridors, such as Nikolai Miliutin and Ivan Leonidov.[2] The second group offered what Sabsovich decried as automobile socialism; they envisioned services and employment extending along efficient road systems linked by fast, flexible, and individually operated transportation. Although the Californization of the Soviet hinterlands has never taken place, the demands of these "deurbanists" for population ceilings, functional zoning, residential superblocks—or microdistricts as the Soviets call them—and new town development all came to be incorporated into Soviet holy writ.[3]

Soviet architectural historians tend to view discussions of the 1920s as involving a conflict between traditionalists, on the one hand, and rationalists and constructivists, on the other.[4] Led by Aleksei Shchusev and Leontii Benois, the traditionalists sought to further develop universal architectural traditions. These architects—and their organizations such as the Moscow Architectural Society (Moskovskoe arkhitekturnoe obshchestvo, or MAO), the Petrograd Society of Architects (Petrogradskoe obshchestvo arkhitektorov), and the Society of Architect-Artists (Obshchestvo arkhitektorov-khudozhnikov)—attempted to improve past practices rather than abandon them.

According to Soviet specialists, two groups of younger architects opposed the traditionalists and demanded completely new approaches to the organization of urban space. Led by such figures as the Vesnin brothers, the Golosov brothers, Moisei Ginzburg, Nikolai Ladovskii, and Konstantin Melnikov at the State Higher Art and Technical Studios (Vkhutemas), these innovators enjoyed considerable success with their designs for exhibition pavilions, workers' clubs, local municipal and Communist Party centers, and other public structures.[5] They, in turn, were divided. On the one hand stood the rationalists, such as Ladovskii and his colleagues at the Association of New Architects (Assotsiatsiia novykh arkhitektorov, or Asnova), who attempted to establish new building forms based on "objective" laws. On the other, the constructivists, led by the Vesnin brothers, the Golosov brothers, Moisei Ginzburg, and Ivan Leonidov at the Association of Contemporary Architects (Obedinenie sovremennykh arkhitektorov, or OSA), advocated the creation of new building forms through their designs as well as in the pages of their association's journal, *Sovremennaia arkhitektura* (Contemporary architecture). These architects focused their attention primarily on implementing the technical and functional aspects of the design process.[6] Some Soviet historians now claim that the traditionalists supported their more radical junior partners. Nevertheless, in the end, the effort to create a new architecture was doomed to failure, for it could not satisfy the social demands generated by the industrialization drives of the 1930s.

Throughout the 1920s considerable sentiment favored discarding the city as a fundamental unit of social and economic organization. This hostility toward the city became manifest in an early adherence to modernism and, as such, can be linked to similar developments in Europe and North America. Le Corbusier, Ernst May, and Mart Stam were all active in the Soviet Union during the period, and Vasili Kandinskii's activities at the Bauhaus further integrated Russian architects into the mainstream of the modernist movement.[7]

Few of the more radical proposals from the 1920s ever left the drawing board. Not only were the necessary financial and human resources in critically short supply, but the workers for whom many of the most original projects were designed remained leery of collective living arrangements. Once rapid industrialization became the state's primary objective, most Communist Party leaders lost whatever interest they may have had in futuristic architecture. With tens of thousands of peasants streaming into the cities each day, expediency dictated an urban solution to the debate over the character of socialist cities. As mentioned in Chapter 1, Lazar Kaganovich brought the antiurbanist revolt to a sudden end in 1931 with an address declaring that the nationalization of private property had made all Soviet cities socialist by definition.[8] He warned that the party would consider any effort to dispute such a position by advocating the abandonment of the city nothing less than sabotage.

Within a few years, city planning and architectural institutes and schools opened—or were reopened—across the Soviet Union. The formation of the Moscow Architectural Institute (Moskovskii arkhitekturnyi institut) in 1933 from the sectors remaining from the prerevolutionary Moscow School of Painting, Sculpture, and Architecture (Moskovskoe uchilishche zhivopisi, vaianiia i zodchestva), the creation of the USSR Academy of Architecture (Akademiia arkhitektury SSSR) in 1934, and the convening of the first congress of the USSR Union of Architects in 1937, represent watersheds in the reinstitutionalization of the profession. (The Union itself was founded in 1932 as the Soiuz sovetskikh arkhitektorov; the organization's present name is Soiuz arkhitektorov SSSR.) During the 1930s, comprehensive plans were unveiled for the reconstruction and expansion of Moscow, Leningrad, Kharkov, Minsk, Tashkent, and numerous other cities as well as for several totally new regional and republican capitals.[9] The prerevolutionary classical revival also had a significant influence on the new images of a socialist urban future (Fig.

58), but this infusion of classical design with socialist values was frequently realized through extravagant and unprincipled use of decoration. As has been noted, the result was a pseudoclassicism that would continue to dominate Soviet urban and architectural design until the death of General Secretary Joseph Stalin in 1953. Meanwhile, the Soviet avant-garde passed into history.

A score or more structures from the revolutionary years of the 1920s remain in old Moscow neighborhoods—striking anomalies in an increasingly monotonous cityscape. They represent a brief period in Russian architectural history during which the quest for a synthesis between structure and decoration begun during the mid-nineteenth century—as discussed by William C. Brumfield in Chapter 2—looked forward to an international revolutionary future rather than backward to a lost national style. Function conquered decoration—although not the Russian love for asymmetry—as new technologies combined with Bolshevik faith in an industrial future to create a number of highly idiosyncratic

58 Apartment house, Marx Prospekt. Moscow. 1934. Architect: Ivan Zholtovskii. Photo: William Brumfield.

structures. This chapter explores the work of the generation of architects that followed those discussed in Chapter 2. These buildings, selected for their artistic and historical significance, bear witness to the vitality of the 1920s as well as to the various competing styles of the period. Readers who wish to see these structures should note that all of them are accessible from the center of Moscow by foot or subway.

KONSTANTIN MELNIKOV:
WESTERN ADMIRERS AND SOVIET CRITICS

During the 1920s, Konstantin Melnikov was perhaps the best-known Soviet avant-garde architect. The son of peasant migrants to Moscow's factories, Melnikov attended the prestigious Moscow School of Painting, Sculpture, and Architecture with the financial assistance of the prominent Moscow engineer Vladimir Chaplin, and graduated from there in 1917.[10] Melnikov's classical training is reflected in his first project—the facade of the main building of the AMO Automobile Factory (1917; now Moscow's Likhachev Automobile Factory). By contrast, his 1923 Makhorka Pavilion at the First All-Union Agricultural and Cottage Industries Exposition used wood construction, multicolored graphics, exposed interiors and the play of planes and acute angles to striking effect.

Melnikov gained international recognition when his Soviet Pavilion at the 1925 International Exposition of Decorative Arts in Paris, a structure that exhibited the same expressionist approach to design evident in his Makhorka Pavilion, was awarded the highest prize for pavilion design. In 1927, he was honored by being the lone Soviet architect to be given his own section at the Machine Age Exposition in New York, and in 1933, the Fifth Milan Trienalle listed him among the world's great living architects. (Others similarly honored included Le Corbusier, Loos, Mendelsohn, Mies van der Rohe, Gropius, and Wright.) It was during this period that the Western architectural community began to take note of what was happening in Soviet Russia.

Nevertheless, by the early 1930s Melnikov was already being attacked by his fellow Soviet architects and by the Communist Party for his "self-love and egotism," "morose fantasies," and "formalism"—the last being a sin because it demonstrated less enthusiasm for encouraging fundamental economic and social change than for altering the outward trappings of life. Denounced at the First All-Union Congress of Soviet Architects in 1937, Melnikov was denied the right to practice his profession. He lived long enough to be redis-covered by a later generation of Soviet architects, and in 1965 was feted with a banquet held at the Union of Soviet Ar-chitects in honor of his seventy-fifth birthday. Melnikov died quietly in 1974.

59 Melnikov house. Moscow. 1927–29. Archi-tect: Konstantin Melnikov. View from Krivoarbat-skii Lane. Photo: William Brumfield.

Melnikov's house, located near the Old Arbat on a small side street, is a remarkable design consisting of two inter-secting cylinders in a brilliant yet surprisingly simple use of interior space and natural lighting.[11] In addition to a glass wall facing Krivoarbatskii Lane and crowned with the inscrip-tion "Konstantin Melnikov, Architect," Melnikov placed elongated hexagonal windows throughout the surface of the rear cylinder, which resembles a medieval fortress tower (Figs. 59, 60). These windows are notable for the manner in which they maximize interior lighting in a gloomy clime and frame the parklike setting of the house. (Melnikov's house provides a rare example of a house occupying an open lot in central Moscow.) In 1936, Karo Alabian, the Armenian architect who was to lead the attack on Melnikov at the First All-Union Congress of Soviet Architects the following year, concluded that Melnikov's primary ambition—and, for Alabian, principal sin—was to create a bold and unusual architecture never before seen or built. And, indeed, Melnikov's

60 Melnikov house. Back facade. Photo: William Brumfield.

house lends some credibility to Alabian's diatribe, for it is one of the most unique domestic structures of this or any century.

Melnikov is also known for his workers' clubs, including the Kauchuk Club on Pliushchika Street (Fig. 61). Built in 1927 for the Union of Chemical Workers as well as for the employees of the Kauchuk Rubber Plant, the club was one of six clubs constructed between 1927 and 1929 according to Melnikov designs. Such clubs were developed by Soviet trade unions during the 1920s in order to provide cultural and educational centers in the hope that such facilities would help to instill a proper revolutionary consciousness while simultaneously combating alcoholism.[12] The Soviet Union's continuing high rate of alcohol consumption suggests that the clubs may have failed in their stated task. There is considerable evidence, however, that they came to serve as much-needed community centers. Their innovative role in Russian life stimulated a need for new spatial forms, and consequently, the sponsoring unions frequently gave their commissions to the era's avant-garde architects, such as Melnikov. The architects, in turn, relished the opportunity to apply their theories to practical situations.

The Kauchuk Club structure itself offers a classical symmetry and elegance for a rather small structure confined to an odd-shaped lot. The floor plan links a semicircle and a triangle to dramatic effect, while the club's external staircase leading up to a second floor entrance recalls the main entries to medieval Russian churches. This is a theme repeated in several Melnikov structures, for he believed that such entrances lent a building drama and dynamism.

Melnikov's preference for multilevel entries is even more apparent in his Rusakov Club, which offers the boldest statement of the new order in Russian architecture and life. Indeed, during the late 1920s, a photograph of this club reputedly graced the most popular Moscow postcard. It remains an extremely controversial building even to this day. Much

61   Kauchuk Club. Moscow. 1927. Architect: Konstantin Melnikov. Photo: Blair Ruble.

praised in radical Western architectural publications at the time of its construction, the Rusakov Club became the central focus of attacks on its architect less than a decade later. The club's sharply articulated exterior, which stands as an expression of its interior, is broken by two typical Melnikov devices: external staircases and spacious terraces (Figs. 62, 63). To these well-known Melnikov features have been added pow-

62 Rusakov Club. Moscow. 1927–29. Architect: Konstantin Melnikov. Photo: Blair Ruble.

erful projections making the building's already strong geometric statement of structure even more powerful. Internally, the basic triangular shape was thought to provide better acoustics inasmuch as the hall resembles a large megaphone. The club's auditorium accommodates 1,200 persons and can be subdivided into four smaller rooms holding audiences of between 120 and 360. The building's dynamic impact is reinforced by its height, which makes it visible from great distances even today, when the original wooden houses have been replaced by much larger prefabricated brick high-rises.

Melnikov was not alone in his use of trade union commissions to explore the practical boundaries of his theoretical approaches to socialist architecture. Ilia Golosov's Zuev Club, for example, is similarly striking for its play of geometric forms and innovative use of new construction materials. Ilia Golosov and his elder brother Panteleimon Golosov both became active members of the Moscow avant-garde.[13] Panteleimon graduated from the Moscow School of Painting, Sculpture, and Architecture in 1911, where he and his brother had studied in classes with Melnikov. Panteleimon's style

63 Rusakov Club. Moscow. Detail. Photo: William Brumfield.

remained more rationalistic than that of his brother, as evidenced by his design for the monumental *Pravda* building (1930–35), relatively near the Zuev Club, at 24 Pravda Street. Initially working in the tradition of Russian classicism, Ilia gradually joined the ranks of the avant-garde while teaching with El Lissitzky, Moisei Ginzburg, Nikolai Ladovskii, and his old schoolmate Konstantin Melnikov at Vkhutemas. By the early 1930s, the Golosovs had once again reverted to the precepts of the classical tradition in which they were trained.

The Zuev Club reflects Ilia Golosov's fascination with form and shape. Despite lack of proper maintenance, the striking intersection of concrete rectangles and glass cylinders continues to impress, for it offers a clear example of the sculptural possibilities of architecture seldom matched in twentieth-century Moscow (Figs. 64, 65). Originally constructed amid wooden houses, Ilia Golosov's initial vision has been largely overwhelmed by the surrounding nondescript modern apartment complexes and office blocks.

The Golosov brothers were joined by the fraternal team of Leonid Vesnin, Viktor Vesnin, and Aleksandr Vesnin, who were born to middle-class parents concerned with nurturing an interest in the arts. Viktor and Aleksandr attended St. Petersburg's Institute of Civil Engineering during the early years of this century, whereas their brother studied at the St. Petersburg Academy of Arts with Leontii Benois. Many of their most important commissions were undertaken jointly, for their skills were complementary. Leonid was the more academic in style and outlook; Viktor, the more analytical; and Aleksandr, a successful stage designer, the more artistic.[14] Although prior to World War I the Vesnins had produced unexceptional structures in the style of the Russian neoclassical revival (see Chapter 3), they later became closely identified with constructivism and with the avant-garde OSA, where Aleksandr served as chairman from 1925 until 1930. During the late 1910s, the brothers accepted several industrial projects. As their work in factory design evolved, the Vesnins began to experiment with the use of reinforced concrete; this experimentation complemented their concern with problems of lighting by enabling them to remove internal structural walls. This willingness to experiment, combined with the overall revolutionary spirit of the times, led the Vesnins to produce some of the most important designs of the period. Their entry in the 1922 Palace of Labor competition marked the emergence of full-fledged constructivist architecture in Soviet Russia. Similar to the design submitted by Walter

Gropius and Max Taut for the Chicago *Tribune* competition the same year, the Vesnin's Palace of Labor entry was marked by an absence of decorative ornamentation. Through the use of bold geometric forms and industrial ferroconcrete, the Vesnin brothers sought to make a statement on new mass democratic values.

During the same period, Leonid Vesnin taught at both the Moscow Higher Technical School and the Moscow Architectural Institute. A few years after his death in 1933, his

64   Zuev Club. Moscow. 1927–29. Architect: Ilia Golosov. Photo: William Brumfield.

younger brothers were denounced for their "purism." Viktor acknowledged his errors at the First All-Union Congress of Soviet Architects, and both he and Aleksandr continued to practice architecture for the remainder of their lives. Viktor served as president of the USSR Union of Architects (1939–49) and became a full member of the USSR Academy of Sciences (1943–50). Aleksandr continued his work in stage

65   Zuev Club.
Photo: William
Brumfield.

design as well as teaching and became a member of the Academy of Construction and Architecture in 1956.

The Vesnins were never dogmatic in their experimentation. For example, their design for the enormous Kharkov state theater (1930) demonstrated a flowing elegance absent in many other designs of the period. (Once the Ukrainian capital moved to Kiev, those plans were shelved.) Among the Vesnin brothers' most important structures were the Dnieper Hydroelectric Station (1927–32)—the largest dam in the world at the time of its construction—the ZIL Automobile

Factory Club in Moscow (1937: Fig. 66), the Cinema Actors' Theater (Fig. 67), and the Moscow Trade Department Store. Even in comparison with the Vesnins' entry for the 1922 Palace of Labor competition, the Cinema Actors' Theater is striking for its absence of external ornamentation and its use of ferroconcrete. Although its facade has been altered and obscured by later buildings apparently constructed for precisely that purpose, the Cinema Actors' Theater maintains the clarity of its modernist form.

The trapezoidal Moscow Trade Department Store, which opened on the tenth anniversary of the Bolshevik Revolution, symbolized the material progress brought about by the new socialist order. This three-story structure, extensively modernized during the late 1970s, retains its original creative use of geometric forms, concrete, and glass (Fig. 68). Its ground-to-roof glass curtain wall is of particular significance. The Vesnins may have been influenced here by Walter Gropius's Bauhaus, which was just being completed as they began their design. The department store also resembles the Hallidie Building, constructed in San Francisco a decade before. The Moscow building's glass wall is even more pronounced than that of its distant California cousin, however, because the Vesnins did not add the fanciful cast-iron decoration found on its American counterpart.

TECHNOLOGICAL PROLETARIAN CULTURE

Workers' clubs and department stores sought to capture in concrete and glass a new culture for the masses that many in the 1920s viewed as one of the most public manifestations of the socialist revolution of 1917. Marxist revolutionary culture proclaimed a foundation of scientific principles embodied in dialectical materialism and emphasized innovative technologies in shaping the life and mentality of the proletariat. Three

66 ZIL Automobile Factory Club. Moscow. 1937. Architects: Vesnin Brothers.

prominent structures—the Moscow Planetarium, the Shabolovka Radio Tower, and the Udarnik Movie Theater—
capture this enthusiasm for a technologically inspired socialist
culture that lasted throughout the decade of the 1920s.

Mikhail Barshch and Mikhail Siniavskii's planetarium represented the epitome of the new scientific culture of the 1920s.
Barshch and Siniavskii studied together at Vkhutemas and
became founding members of the constructivist OSA. They
first collaborated on a joint diploma project for a food market
with a design that appeared in *Sovremennaia arkhitektura* in
1928. The year before, they had entered a joint project in the

67 Cinema Ac-
tors' Theater.
Moscow. 1931–
34. Architects:
Vesnin Brothers.
Photo: William
Brumfield.

68 Moscow Trade De-
partment Store. 1927. Ar-
chitects: Vesnin Brothers.
Photo: Blair Ruble.

Sverdlovsk House of Industry competition. The Moscow Planetarium (1928), however, represents their first completed project.[15] Mikhail Barshch eventually became a leading city planner and architectural instructor. In 1929 and 1930, he worked with his former teacher, Moisei Ginzburg, on the Green City Project. (See Chapter 5.) This plan developed the principles for linear cities designed to accommodate one hundred thousand residents in parallel recreational, housing, transportation, and industrial zones—a system developed further by El Lissitzky and Nikolai Miliutin.[16] Barshch also participated in the preparation of plans for Magnitogorsk—one of the most important city-planning and town-building projects of the first Five-Year Plan (1928–1932). Barshch's initial interest in city planning grew out of his concern to develop communal housing structures that would foster a "socialist identity" and a harmonious relationship between urban man and nature. During the three decades following the mid-1930s, Barshch was increasingly involved with city planning (he designed Moscow's Lenin Prospekt in 1950–58) and with his teaching duties at the Moscow Architectural Institute, where he had become a professor in 1935.

Barshch and Siniavskii's planetarium gained immediate recognition. Senior Communist Party leaders endowed the planetarium with considerable ideological significance, for it was to be a new form of educational institution for the masses. The architects attempted to create a design symbolizing the unity between science and entertainment, a structure at once instantly recognizable yet innovative. Their elongated flying-saucer-shaped dome, which is only four centimeters thick at its peak, both achieved that goal and provided commodious surroundings for this "theater without an audience."

The airways joined the cosmos in the Bolshevik imagination, as radio sought to capture and transmit the radical fervor of the period. Built to transmit Radio Comintern's revolutionary message to the farthest reaches of the capitalist world, the distinctive conical structure of the Shabolovka Radio Tower (1922) was designed by the engineer Vladimir Shukhov (see Chapter 2) and soars 160 meters high over what had been a district of largely one-story wooden structures.[17] In its day, this marriage of engineering technique and architectural design symbolized the revolutionary future.

The Udarnik Movie Theater, located next to the government apartment building ("House on the embankment") on a small island in the Moscow River, opened at the end of a remarkable decade that had been launched by broadcasts from

Shabolovka. The completion of this structure marks the conclusion of the avant-garde period in Moscow. Indeed, its
architect, Boris Iofan, eventually came to represent a quite
different tradition in Soviet architecture.[18] Born in Odessa a
year after Melnikov, Iofan studied at the Moscow Higher
Institute of Art, graduating in 1919, and at the engineering
faculty of the University of Rome, where he lived until returning to the Soviet Union in 1924. Among his earliest
commissions were housing projects along Rusakov Street
(1926), near Melnikov's Rusakov Club.

Unlike many of the architects discussed so far, Iofan easily
made the transition to Stalin's preferred classical-romantic
style, as seen in the architect's Soviet pavilions at the world
fairs in Paris (1937) and New York (1939), as well as in his
megalomanic winning design for the 1932 Palace of Soviets
competition. Iofan's Palace of Soviets—which was designed
in conjunction with Vladimir Shchuko and Vladimir Gelfreikh—sported a 415-meter tower crowned by an 80-meter
statue of Lenin. The resulting cylindrical skyscraper was intended to dwarf the Empire State Building. It epitomized the
grandiose and heroic "wedding-cake-gothic" style that soon
replaced the humanistic radical spirit of Moscow's 1920s.[19]

Iofan's tendency toward gigantism is all too apparent in
his Udarnik Movie Theater (Fig. 69). The structure, adjoin-
ing an enormous housing project designed for the elite of the
period by the same architect, is distinguished by a silver barrel
roof reminiscent of Ilia Golosov's constructivist design submitted for the 1923 Moscow Palace of Labor competition.
Opened in 1931 on the fourteenth anniversary of the Bolshevik Revolution, the Udarnik was hailed as the first totally
"Soviet" movie house in Moscow; the structure and all of
its equipment were produced within the Soviet Union. With
more than sixteen hundred seats, the Udarnik was the largest
movie theater in the Soviet Union at the time of its opening.
Like Shchusev's Hotel Moskva (Fig. 70) and Arkadi Langman's Gosplan Building on Marx Prospekt (1936; Fig. 71),
Iofan's Udarnik Movie Theater expresses a new monumen-
talism alien to the avant-garde spirit of the previous decade.

SOCIALIST HOUSING FOR PROLETARIAN HEROES

The new Bolshevik culture sought to redesign not only workers' leisure and labor but also the worker's home, since many
designs during the 1920s were intended to restructure family

life. The work of Moisei Ginzburg, for example, offered a radically new concept of housing.[20] Like Melnikov, the Golosov brothers, and the Vesnins, Ginzburg, a native of Minsk, was trained in the classical tradition. He graduated with a degree in architecture from L'Academie des beaux-arts in Milan in 1914 and a degree in engineering from the Riga Polytechnical Institute in 1917. In 1921, he traveled to Moscow and launched his affiliation with that city's architectural community. In 1923, Ginzburg became head of the Faculty of Architectural History at Vkhutemas, and taught at the Moscow Institute of Higher Technology as well. He remained active in architectural debates, establishing himself as a major theoretician with the appearance of his *Rhythm in Architecture* (1923) and *Style and the Epoch* (1924).[21] A member of the Russian Academy of Artistic Studies (Rakhin), Ginzburg became a founding member of the OSA and a leading editor of *Sovremennaia arkhitektura*.

Over the course of the 1920s, Ginzburg's interest evolved

69 Udarnik Movie Theater. Moscow. 1928–31. Architect: Boris Iofan. Photo: William Brumfield.

70   Hotel Moskva. Moscow. 1935. Architect: Aleksei Shchusev. Photo: William Brumfield.

71   Gosplan Building. Moscow. 1935. Architect: Arkadii Langman. Photo: William Brumfield.

from a preoccupation with problems of architectural composition and style to an emerging concern with functional design and social problems. He submitted plans to nearly every major competition of the period, and his designs for the Court of Justice in Alma-Ata (1927–30)—currently part of the Kazakh State University—and a Crimean resort were eventually constructed. His most famous project—the Narkomfin (People's Commissariat of Finance) Housing Commune—still stands near the current United States Embassy on Chaikovskii Street, although it has been obscured by more recent construction.

The Narkomfin Housing Commune, built by Ginzburg and Ignati Milinis, reflected a growing concern for the social consequences of architecture. The five-story design consisted of separate dwelling, community, service, and children's units and included structural elements popular at the time both in the USSR and abroad: a glass "curtain wall," ribbon windows, and standardized floor plans (Fig. 72). The Narkomfin Housing Commune was intended to restructure social relationships along communal lines. The architects compressed interior layouts by reducing individualized service areas to an absolute minimum, particularly kitchen and bath facilities. Nevertheless, they sought to maximize the psychological space of each unit by dividing it among several levels. The resulting small—on average thirty square meters—duplexes and triplexes proved remarkably innovative. Indeed, they appear to have been rediscovered four decades later on a larger scale by Moshe Safdie in his "Habitat" at the Montreal Expo '67 and his Coldspring New Town development in Baltimore.

72 Narkomfin Housing Commune. Moscow. 1928–30. Architects: Moisei Ginzburg, Ignatii Milinis. Photo: William Brumfield.

Not content to create a new environment on Moscow's pe-
riphery, the avant-garde also attempted to rebuild the city's
main street—Tverskaia Street (now Gorkii Street). One such
effort, prominent for its central location and distinctive facade, was the seven-story *Izvestiia* building designed by Grigorii Barkhin. Barkhin was born in the Urals and graduated
in 1908 from the Academy of Arts in St. Petersburg.[22] The
following year he traveled to Moscow, where he began a
forty-four-year teaching career, much of which was spent at
what would eventually become the Moscow Architectural
Institute. By the late 1920s, Barkhin was in joint practice
with his son, Mikhail—a collaboration that lasted more than
a quarter century.

Barkhin's most significant contributions came in theater
design and city planning. His plans for the Dnepropetrovsk
Palace of Culture (1925), the Rostov-on-Don Theater (1930),
and the Sverdlovsk Theater (1932) made imaginative use of
form and space. These designs demonstrate a familiarity with
the innovative theaters of early twentieth-century Europe.
Barkhin's Sverdlovsk Theater design was among the most
advanced of its era, accommodating audiences ranging from
four thousand to nine thousand persons depending upon the
nature of the performance. The architect's interest in theater
design is further evident in his monograph, *The Architecture
of the Theater,* published in 1947.

With the emergence of classicism in Soviet architecture
following the 1932 Palace of Soviets competition, Barkhin
increasingly devoted himself to problems of urban design.
His interest was hardly new, for he was an early advocate of
proletarian garden cities. From 1933 until 1937 he participated
in efforts to formulate a redevelopment plan for the city of
Moscow, heading a group of planners responsible for the
Dzerzhinskii district *(raion)*. After the Second World War,
Barkhin prepared the Sevastopol Reconstruction Plan (1944–
47). He continued to practice as an urban planner until shortly
before his death in 1969.

In many ways, the *Izvestiia* building is less interesting
than Barkhin's work in theater design and city planning.
Nonetheless, its prominent location in the capital has
placed this structure among the most widely recognized
constructivist buildings of the period (Fig. 73). The *Izvestiia* building is noteworthy for its external statement of internal structure, its use of facade screening devices

(primarily balconies), its repetition of the cube shape, and its aesthetically advanced combination of cement, steel, and glass. The *Izvestiia* building remains one of the most forceful statements of the constructivist concern for form, structure, and rational design.

A few blocks from Barkhin's *Izvestiia* building stands the Institute of Marxism-Leninism, designed by Sergei Chernyshev.[23] A student of the prominent architect-teacher Leontii Benois, Chernyshev graduated in 1907 from the Academy of Arts in St. Petersburg. During the early Soviet period, Chernyshev taught at Vkhutemas and joined with Leonid Vesnin to win one of the Soviet Union's first major architectural competitions, held in 1922, for the Serpukhov Street Workers' Housing District. Chernyshev later taught at the Moscow Architectural Institute (1933–50) and served as chief architect of Moscow (1934–41), chairman of the Architectural Administration of the Moscow City Soviet (1944–48), as well as first secretary of the USSR Union of Architects (1950–51). He was also a prominent member of the architectural team responsible for designing the buildings constructed on the Lenin Hills for Moscow State University (1949–53).

Chernyshev's headquarters for the newly created Lenin Institute—a design that he developed in conjunction with Lev Rudnev, Pavel Abrosimov, and Aleksandr Khriakov—opened on November 7, 1926, the ninth anniversary of the Bolshevik Revolution. The complex includes a five-story rectangular building visible from Soviet Square on Gorkii Street, as well as a less prominent fifteen-story tower. Its simplicity achieves a human scale and a general austerity that contrasts with the heroic mission of the institution it was designed to house. The small park in front of the institute combines with the pastel green of the exterior walls to create a peaceful effect.

Further down Gorkii Street in the direction of the Kremlin is the Central Telegraph Building designed by Ivan Rerberg.[24] Rerberg represents a generation that taught many of the avant-garde architects of the 1920s. An 1896 graduate of the St. Petersburg Academy of Military Engineering, Rerberg returned to his native Moscow to teach at the Moscow School of Painting, Sculpture, and Architecture from 1906 until 1919. During this period, he designed several neoclassical buildings in Moscow and, together with Viacheslav Oltarzhevskii, the city's Kiev Station, a building discussed in Chapter 3. Aside from the Central Telegraph Building, Rerberg

73 (facing page) *Izvestiia* building. Moscow. 1927. Architects: Grigorii and Mikhail Barkhin. Photo: William Brumfield.

133

is known for housing projects, as well as for the School of Red Commandants (1932–34), currently used by the Presidium of the USSR Supreme Soviet.

The competition for the Central Telegraph Building specified that the structure should reflect its industrial and public functions as well as serve as a major monument to the newly emerging "Red Moscow." Numerous architects submitted constructivist designs maximizing exposed steel, cement, and glass. Although it evokes a more classical spirit, Rerberg's building uses many of these features as well. This scent of classicism led Moscow's modernists to savagely attack the winning design. Nevertheless, the telegraph office, which opened in 1927 on the tenth anniversary of the Bolshevik Revolution, is typical of the era that produced it and continues to function as the primary intercity and international telephone, telegraph, and postal office for central Moscow.

MOSCOW'S NEW RED GATEWAY

Less than two miles to the northeast of Rerberg's Central Telegraph Building, at the intersection of Kirov and Sadovaia-Spasskaia streets, lie the remnants of what was to have replaced Gorkii Street as the major boulevard running toward the Kremlin. Here, within a few hundred meters of each other, stand three of the most important buildings constructed in Moscow during the 1920s. These buildings—Le Corbusier's Central Consumers' Union Building (1928–35), Boris Velikovskii's State Trade Offices (1925–27), and Aleksei Shchusev's Ministry of Agriculture (1928–33)—were intended to provide a triumphant new entrance to socialist Moscow.

Le Corbusier (Charles-Eduard Jeanneret) traveled to Moscow in 1928, a year after he had been excluded from the League of Nations competition in Geneva for failing to use India ink in his submissions. In Moscow his design proposal won the competition for the Central Consumers' Union Building (Tsentrosoiuz), constructed from 1928 to 1935. Le Corbusier arrived in Moscow at a time when his reputation as an innovator had already been firmly established through his association with the Parisian avant-garde review *L'Esprit nouveau,* and his efforts to create the International Congresses of Modern Architecture (CIAM).[25] After Moscow, he went on his famous Latin American tour, which led to his building design for the Brazilian Ministry of Education and Health in Rio de Janeiro (1936) and his Buenos Aires Master Plan (1938).

The Central Consumers' Union Building—currently the headquarters of the Central Statistical Administration—is one of the most important examples of 1920s modernism to be found anywhere. Its design closely follows Le Corbusier's proposal for the League of Nations building in Geneva, a plan that has set the tone for buildings housing international organizations ever since. The Central Consumers' Union Building featured a segregation of function into distinct structures linked together at key points (Fig. 74). Le Corbusier's concern for classical proportions combined here with a massive articulation of geometric forms to create a new utilitarian aesthetic. Further along Kirov Street, opposite the corner of Kirov Lane, stands Velikovskii's State Trade (Gostorg) Building.[26] In viewing this austere seven-story glass and concrete structure, it is important to remember that the current building (woefully maintained) was intended to serve as a pedestal for a much taller glass office tower (Fig. 75). The

74 Tsentrosoiuz Building. Moscow. 1928–35. Architect: Le Corbusier. Photo: Blair Ruble.

Gostorg Building illustrates the unfulfilled promise of the Moscow avant-garde—particularly in its innovative use of glass walls and partitions.

The last of the three modernist structures in the Kirov area is the headquarters building of the USSR Ministry of Agriculture, designed in 1928 by Aleksei Shchusev. From 1891 until 1897, Shchusev studied painting at the Academy of Arts in St. Petersburg.[27] By the outbreak of the First World War, he had already developed a reputation as a leading figure in

75   Gostorg Building. Moscow. 1925–27. Architect: Boris Velikovskii. Photo: Blair Ruble.

the artistic and architectural worlds of Moscow for his work in designing churches using a modernized interpretation of medieval architecture. A traditionalist by inclination as well as training, Shchusev's early work was influenced by his extensive archaeological research. His primary prewar architectural projects—the picturesque neo-Muscovite Kazan Station on Komsomol Square (1911–26) and his Church of the Intercession of the Virgin of the Marfo-Mariinskii Convent on Bolshaia Ordinka Street (1908–11)—reflect his interest in historical themes.

Shchusev flourished in the immediate postrevolutionary period. In 1922, he became president of the Moscow Architectural Society (MAO) and taught for some time at Vkhutemas. By 1924 he was a leading member of a team of architects charged by the Moscow city soviet with preparing a new general development plan for the city. That effort, called the "New Moscow" Project (Proekt "Novaia Moskva"), involved many of the period's prominent architects: Shchusev, Ivan Zholtovskii, Leonid Vesnin, Ilia Go-

76 Ministry of Agriculture. Moscow. 1928. Architect: Aleksei Shchusev. Photo: William Brumfield.

losov, Nikolai Dokuchaev, Nikolai Kolli, Boris Korshunov, Nikolai Ladovskii, Konstantin Melnikov, Edgar Norvert, and Sergei Chernyshev. Their effort conformed to the tenor of the times by proposing the total redesign and modernization of the central city. Shchusev's duties as director of the Tretiakov Gallery in Moscow from 1926 until 1929 also allowed him to promote the work of more radical junior architects such as those involved in the "New Moscow" Project.

Most of his own "modern" structures retained classical lines and proportions, stripped of ornamentation. This approach is apparent in Shchusev's design for the permanent granite Lenin Mausoleum on Red Square (1930), which was itself patterned on the temporary wooden structures that he had designed to inter Lenin's remains in 1924. Shchusev's essentially classical orientation led him to develop the so-called Red doric style, which retained visible external columns without capitals. Shchusev adapted easily to the emer-

77 Lenin State Library. Moscow. 1928–40. Architects: Vladimir Shchuko, V. Gelfreikh. Photo: William Brumfield.

138

gence of Stalinist neoclassicism during the 1930s, as seen in his design for the Hotel Moskva on Manezh Square (1930–35). By the mid-1930s, he was attacking many of the younger architects whose careers he had supported during the previous decade. Nonetheless, he retained his status of "grandfather" to the profession, serving from 1946 until his death in 1949 as director of the National Architectural Museum—an institution that now bears his name. Among his many honors, Shchusev was elected a member of the USSR Academy of Sciences in 1943.

78   Ministry of Foreign Affairs. Moscow. 1954. Architects: M. Minkus, V. Gelfreikh. Photo: William Brumfield.

The most striking feature of Shchusev's Ministry of Agriculture building is that it bears virtually no resemblance to his other work (Fig. 76). Instead, this structure combines features of many of the other buildings being constructed during the same period: the cylinder of Golosov's Zuev Club, the balconies and clock of Barkhin's *Izvestiia* building, and the pattern of glass and concrete of Velikovskii's Gostorg Office. The derivative nature of the design is offset by the architect's sensitive use of proportion and color.

79   Moscow State University. Lenin Hills, Moscow. 1947–54. Architect: Lev Rudnev. Photo: William Brumfield.

The fervor for innovation in Russian architecture at the beginning of this century had appeared in full force after the Bolshevik Revolution in 1917. The social and political upheavals of revolution and civil war unleashed a quest for the

modern among architects, some of whom appear to have derived new design elements from preclassical Russian forms (compare the second-story entrances to Konstantin Melnikov's workers' clubs and his highly idiosyncratic house design). Other architects remained mesmerized by the aesthetic power of new technologies, as displayed in Mikhail Barshch and Mikhail Siniavskii's planetarium and in Vladimir Shukhov's Shabolovka Radio Tower. Finally, visionaries looked to their Western counterparts for inspiration, as did Velikovskii with his truncated Gostorg skyscraper, which would have rivaled the towers of Chicago and New York had it been completed. And the intense interest in Western architecture prompted the Central Consumers' Union to invite Le Corbusier to build a variant of his failed proposal from the League of Nations competition in Moscow.

This search for a revolutionary style eroded over the course of the twenties. On the one hand, the proletarian vanguard did not care for the communal housing arrangements proposed by such socialist visionaries as Moisei Ginzburg; on the other, Soviet technology remained too primitive to sustain a radical rebuilding program in Moscow, or elsewhere. After the initial Five-Year Plans of the late 1920s and 1930s set as their goal the rapid transformation of the Soviet Union into an industrial state, architects returned to more monumental forms of a pseudoclassicism preferred by Stalin (Figs. 77, 78, 79). In the wake of their retreat remain scattered reminders of the utopian dreams of a band of architects who sought to do nothing less than transform the manner in which human beings live.

APPENDIX: THE BUILDINGS

The Melnikov House
Konstantin Melnikov, 1927–29
Krivoarbatskii pereulok, 10
(Metro: Smolenskaia)

Kauchuk Club
Konstantin Melnikov, 1927
ul. Pliushchika, 64
(Metro: Park Kul'tury,
Frunzinskaia)

Rusakov Club
Konstantin Melnikov, 1928–29
Stromynka, 10
(Metro: Sokolniki)

Zuev Club
Ilia Golosov, 1927–29
Lesnaia ul., 18
(Metro: Belorusskaia)

Cinema Actors' Theater
Vesnin Brothers, 1931
ul. Vorovskogo, 33
(Metro: Krasnopresnenskaia-
Barrikadnaia)

Moscow State Trade Department
Store
Vesnin Brothers, 1926–27
Krasnopresnenskaia zastava, 48/2
(Metro: Ulitsa 1905 goda)

Narkomfin Housing Commune
Moisei Ginzburg and Ignatii
Milinis, 1928–29
ul. Chaikovskogo, 25
(Courtyard)
(Metro: Krasnopresenskaia-
Barrikadnaia)

Planetarium
Mikhail Barshch and Mikhail
Siniavskii,
1927–29

Sadovaia-Kudrinskaia, 5
(Metro: Krasnopresenskaia-
Barrikadnaia)

Izvestiia building
Grigorii Barkhin, 1925–27
Pushkinskaia ploshchad', 5
(Metro: Pushkinskaia-
Gorkovskaia)

Institute of Marxism-Leninism
Sergei Chernyshev, 1926
Sovetskaia ploshchad'
(Metro: Prospekt Marksa,
Pushkinskaia)

Central Telegraph Building
Ivan Rerberg, 1925–27
ul. Gor'kogo, 7
(Metro: Prospekt Marksa)

Map 3   Moscow.

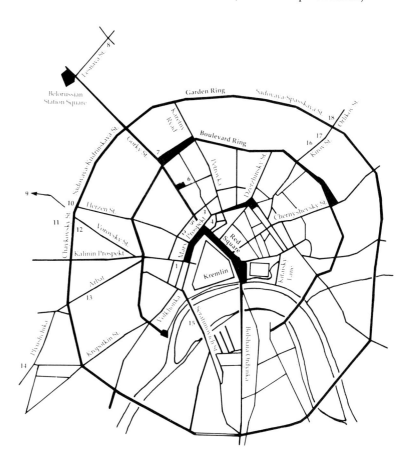

1. Lenin Library
2. Apartment house, Marx Prospekt
3. Gosplan building
4. Hotel Moskva
5. Central Telegraph building
6. Institute of Marxism-Leninism
7. Izvestiia building
8. Zuev Club
9. Mostorg department store
10. Planetarium
11. Narkomfin housing commune
12. Cinema Actors Club
13. Melnikov house
14. Kauchuk Club
15. Udarnik Cinema
16. Tsentrosoiuz building
17. Gostorg building
18. Ministry of Agriculture

Central Consumers' Union
Building
Le Corbusier, 1928–35
ul. Kirova, 39
(Metro: Lermontovskaia,
Kirovskaia)

Gostorg Offices
Boris Velikovskii, 1925–27
ul. Kirova, 47
(Metro: Lermontovskaia,
Kirovskaia)

Ministry of Agriculture
Aleksei Shchusev, 1928–33

Orlikov pereulok, 1/11
(Metro: Lermontovskaia,
Kirovskaia)

Udarnik Movie Theater
Boris Iofan, 1928–31
ul. Serafimovicha, 2
(Metro: Kropotkinskaia, Bibli-
oteka im. Lenina)

Shabolovka Radio Tower
V. Shukhov, 1922
Shabolovka
(Metro: Shabalovskaia)

NOTES

1. For further discussion of these debates, see K. N. Afanas'ev, ed., *Iz istoriia sovetskoi arkhitektury 1926–1932 gg: Dokumenty i materialy*. *Rabochie kluby i dvortsy kul'tury Moskvy* (Moscow: Nauka, 1984); also V. E. Khazanova, ed., *Iz istorii sovetskoi arkhitektury, 1917–1925 gg: Dokumenty i materialy* (Moscow: Akademiia nauk, 1963). A bibliographic listing for the period is contained in Anatole Senkevitch, *Soviet Architecture, 1917–1956: A Bibliographic Guide to Source Material* (Charlottesville: University of Virginia Press, 1973). In English a survey of the competing factions is contained in William C. Brumfield, *Gold in Azure: One Thousand Years of Russian Architecture* (Boston: Godine, 1983), 338–46.

2. Miliutin's work is available in English in Nikolai Miliutin, "Sotsgorod," *The Construction of Socialist Cities* (Cambridge: MIT Press, 1974). Sabsovich's classic study may be found in the Russian-language original in Leonid Sabsovich, *Sotsialisticheskii goroda* (Moscow, 1930). Western views of their works are to be found in Anatole Kopp, *Constructivist Architecture in the USSR* (New York: St. Martin's Press, 1985); and Vladimir Papernyi, *Kultura "Dva"* (Ann Arbor: Ardis, 1985).

3. B. Lunin, ed., *Gorod sotsializma i sotsialisticheskaia rekonstruktsiia byta* (Moscow, 1930); Maurice F. Parkins, *City Planning in Soviet Russia* (Chicago: University of Chicago Press, 1953).

4. See, for example, Selim Omarovich Khan-Magomedov, *Pioneers of Soviet Architecture* (New York: Rizzoli, 1987).

5. The work of these modernists is examined in Anatole Kopp, *Changer la vie, changer la ville: de la vie nouvelle aux problemes urbains, URSS, 1917–1931* (Paris: Union Generale d'Editions, 1975); and, by the same author, *Town and Revolution: Soviet Architecture and City Planning, 1917–1935* (London: Thames and Hudson, 1970).

6. Oleg A. Shvidkovsky, ed., *Building in the USSR, 1917–1932* (London: Studio Vista, 1971), 29–34; Arthur Voyce, *Russian Architecture: Trends in Nationalism and Modernism* (New York: Philosophical Library, 1948), 134–41.

143

7. Catherine Cooke, ed., *Russian Avant-Garde Art and Architecture* (London: Architectural Design, 1983), 50–59; Centre Georges Pompidou, *Catalogue de l'exposition Paris-Moscou* (Paris: Centre Georges Pompidou, 1979), 286–302.

8. L. M. Kaganovich, *Za sotsialisticheskuiu rekonstruktsiiu Moskvy i gorodov SSSR* (Moscow: OGIZ "Moskovskii Rabochii," 1931) p. 73, and Parkins, *City Planning in Soviet Russia*, p. 10.

9. Khan-Magomedov, *Pioneers of Soviet Architecture*.

10. For a detailed analysis of Konstantin Melnikov's work, see Frederick S. Starr, *Melnikov: Solo Architecture in a Mass Society* (Princeton: Princeton University Press, 1978); Khan-Magomedov, *Pioneers of Soviet Architecture*, 551–53; and Shvidokovsky, ed., *Building in the USSR*, 57–66.

11. Melnikov's house is discussed in Starr, *Melnikov*, 117–25; and Brumfield, *Gold in Azure*, 348–50.

12. Workers' clubs in the 1920s are described in Afanas'ev, ed., *Iz istorii sovetskoi arkhitektury;* and Andrei V. Ikonnikov, *Arkhitektura Moskvy XX vek.* (Moscow: Moskovskii rabochii, 1984), 57–66.

13. Additional discussion of the work of the Golosovs may be found in Selim Omarovich Khan-Magomedov, *Il'ia Golosov* (Moscow: Stroiizdat, 1972); Khan-Magomedov, *Pioneers of Soviet Architecture*, 561–64; and Shvidkovsky, ed., *Building in the USSR*, 106–14.

14. Concerning the Vesnins, see Selim Omarovich Khan-Magomedov, *Aleksandr Vesnin and Russian Constructivism* (New York: Rizzoli, 1986); Khan-Magomedov, *Pioneers of Soviet Architecture*, 547–51; and Shvidkovsky, ed., *Building in the USSR*, 42–56.

15. Shvidkovsky, ed., *Building in the USSR*, 97–105.

16. El Lissitzky, *Russia: An Architecture for World Revolution*, trans. Eric Dluhosch (Cambridge: MIT Press, 1982); Miliutin, "Sotsgorod."

17. Shukhov's towers, as well as Vladimir Tatlin's monument to the Third International, are discussed in Ikonnikov, *Arkhitektura Moskvy*, 46.

18. See I. Iu. Eigel', *Boris Iofan* (Moscow: Stroiizdat, 1978).

19. A fresh perspective on this competition is found in Papernyi, *Kultura "Dva"*; and Ikonnikov, *Arkhitektura Moskvy*, 96–104.

20. See Selim Omarovich Khan-Magomedov, *M. A. Ginzburg* (Moscow: Stroiizdat, 1972).

21. For an English translation, see Moisei Ginzburg, *Style and Epoch* (Cambridge: MIT Press, 1982).

22. For a concise English-language review of Barkhin's work, including the *Izvestiia* building, see Shvidkovsky, ed. *Building in the USSR*, 78–86.

23. Iurii Aleksandrov, *Moscow: Past and Present* (Moscow: Raduga, 1984), 175–76.

24. Ibid., 173–74.

25. Also see Robert Fishman, *Urban Utopias in the Twentieth Century: Ebenezer Howard, Frank Lloyd Wright, Le Corbusier* (New York: Basic Books, 1977); Centre Georges Pompidou, *Catalogue de l'exposition Paris-Moscou*; and Dennis Sharp, *Sources of Modern Architecture* (London: Architectural Association, 1967).

26. Ikonnikov, *Arkhitektura Moskvy*, 54.

27. K. N. Afanas'ev, *A. V. Shchusev* (Moscow: Stroiizdat, 1978).

5 THE REALIZATION OF UTOPIA: WESTERN TECHNOLOGY AND SOVIET AVANT-GARDE ARCHITECTURE

Milka Bliznakov

"THE Materialized Utopia" (*Oveshchestvlennaia Uto-piia*) was the title Boris I. Arvatov gave to his polemical defense of innovative and imaginative designs for future cities and housing in the Soviet Union:

Towns of the future have been described also in the past: Moore, Gourier, Morris, etc.

Fourier is a utopian, his utopia is revolutionary. . . .

Who does not know that without Fourier and others, there would not have been Marx? . . .

Towns in the air; towns of glass and asbestos; towns on springs; what are they—eccentricity, tricks, desire to be original? No, they are simply *optimized purposefulness*.

In the air—in order to free the earth.

Made of glass—to be filled with light.

Asbestos—to reduce the structures' weight.

On springs—to achieve balance.[1]

The future seemed within the reach of the present for many social theoreticians, avant-garde artists and architects, and even simple workers. The stimulus for imagining a new future, generated by the Revolution of 1917, continued through the period of the first Five-Year Plan (1928–32). This plan called for "putting into practice all that, until recently, was [considered] fantasy and utopia."[2] A book published in 1932 for children of foreign workers in the USSR told its young readers:

In just one factory in Nizhni Novgorod we expect to build 200,000 automobiles a year. Into Siberian taiga, the Kirgiz steppe, everywhere, the automobile will penetrate. . . . By 1932 we shall have 138 airplanes. It will then be possible to fly from Moscow to Vladivostock and Tashkent, from Novosibirsk to Berlin. . . . Every future city will be a workers' village . . . factories and unions of factories will not be brought together in one center as at present: they will be distributed throughout the entire country according to a rational plan. . . . Socialism is no longer a myth, a fantasy of the mind. We ourselves are building it.[3]

During the decade between the promises of a utopian future in the early 1920s and the actual building of socialism during the 1930s, architects in the Soviet Union created the most imaginative and far-reaching experimental projects in the history of the modern movement. The construction of these projects often required technologies not available at the time in Russia; hence they continued to be considered utopian projects by Soviet and Western scholars. But these projects for cities and buildings were designed to symbolize a new political structure—socialism and communism. This sociopolitical order promised an abundance to be provided by the continuous development of science, technology, and industry. To architects, it seemed that with the state investing in rapid industrial development, these promises could soon be fulfilled.

The keen awareness of the implications of scientific discoveries for a different future gave rise during the 1920s to Soviet science fiction. Numerous novels and short stories explored scientific possibilities and sociopolitical changes in appealing and effective images. Some envisioned utopian futures; others proposed dis-topian options. More than 150 works of science fiction were published in the Soviet Union during the 1920s, an astonishing volume when compared with the limited contribution Russian writers made to science fiction and utopian literature during the nineteenth and early twentieth centuries.[4] Russia's retarded scientific and industrial development and its tradition of realistic and didactic novels had impeded the development of Russian science fiction, with the notable exception of Nikolai Chernyshevskii's utopian *What Is to Be Done?*.[5] Written in prison in 1862, this book by the leader of Russia's radical intelligentsia was republished several times during the 1920s. The physical environment of Chernyshevskii's utopian society resembles Fourier's phalanstery: air-conditioned glass and iron crystal palaces where two thousand people could live, work, study, attend theaters, and visit museums. In addition to this prevailing housing type, however, secluded pavilions and tents for nature lovers and splendid cities for dense urban and cultural life provided choices and variety for the inhabitants. Mechanized farming and industry required little labor, thus leaving ample time for individual and cultural development.

The first avant-garde architectural projects were also phalanstery complexes—for example, Nikolai Ladovskii's Architectural Manifestation of a Communal House of 1920 (Fig. 80). Ladovskii, the founder and spiritual leader of the Association of New Architects (Asnova), displayed his project at the Nineteenth State Exhibition in Moscow. Attached to one of his drawings was a handwritten note stating his personal credo: "Technology creates wonders. Architecture also must create wonders." This drive to parallel the latest technological developments motivated numerous architects to experiment with design, as it motivated writers to describe future environments. Next to Chernyshevskii's novel, the most popular prerevolutionary utopia was by Aleksandr Bogdanov-Malinovskii: *Red Star: A Utopia,* first published in 1908 and reprinted in 1918, 1922, and 1928. A stage version was produced by the Proletkult theater in 1920. Its sequel, *Engineer Menni* (1913), was reprinted at least seven times during the 1920s.[6] Following Chernyshevskii's model, the Martians had choices in work, entertainment, and habitat. Denser urban environments, such as the great City of Machines, alternated with small towns and suburban settlements. The preferred housing, however, was not phalansteries or house-communes, but glass-roofed individual residences spreading throughout continuous parks. Bogdanov's 1907 definition of architecture resembles a constructivist manifesto of the 1920s:

By architecture the Martians mean not only buildings and great works of engineering but also the artistic designing of furniture, tools, machines and all other useful objects and materials. The immense significance of this art in their lives may be judged by the particular care and thoroughness with which the collection [of pictures, drawings, models] was arranged [in their museums]. As on Earth, in the works of earlier periods elegance was often achieved at the expense of comfort, and embellishments impaired serviceability and interfered with the function of objects. I detected nothing of the sort in the art of the contemporary period, either in the furniture, the implements, or the buildings and other structures. I asked . . . whether contemporary architecture permitted deviations from functional perfection for the sake of beauty.

"Never," [the Martian] replied. "That would be false beauty, artificiality rather than art."[7]

The construction of buildings on Mars was industrialized as was the production of clothing, footwear, machinery, and other commodities. Industrial plants were clean and air-

80 Architectural Manifes-
tation of a Communal
House. 1920. Architect:
Nikolai Ladovskii.

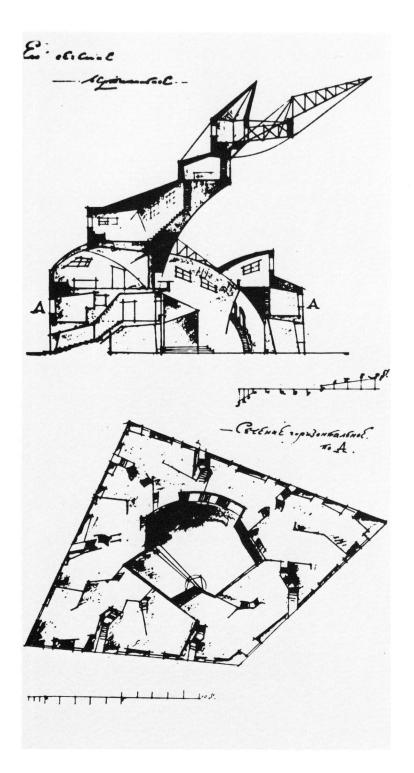

conditioned. Pollution was avoided through the exclusive use of hydroelectric energy. Numerous new inventions contributed to the harmonious synthesis of social organization and humanistic life-style. Bogdanov's works inspired revolutionary sciences and pointed the way for imaginative architects to design structures to help realize his social dreams. For example, Leonard M. Sabsovich, a prophet of speed industrialization and collectivization, proposed in his work *The City of the Future and the Organization of the Socialist Way of Life* (1929) a model for transforming Russia's towns and villages into new socialist towns within fifteen years.[8]

The theme of planetary adventures, a recurring topic in Soviet science fiction, was actually pioneered by Konstantin Tsiolkovskii, a mathematician and researcher in rocketry.[9] *Outside Earth*, his 1912 work of science fiction that was published only in 1918, described rocketship colonies in space. Ten years later, a talented young architect, Georgii T. Krutikov, proposed this theme as his thesis project (Figs. 81, 82). Space colonization was also explored by other Ladovskii students: Viktor P. Kalmykov in his "Saturnii" project of 1928–30 (Fig. 83) and Isaak L. Iuzefovich in the "Aerostad" project of 1926–29.

This burst of creative energy, expressed in literary and architectural images of future life-styles, was promoted and sustained by a revolutionary regime committed to industrialization and modern science. The Soviet Union perceived its role as the transformer of social goals into reality and saw itself as the rightful heir of earlier social reformers. During the years following the revolution, many radicals—socialist, communist, anarchist—believed in an imminent world revolution that would make available for everyone all the latest scientific and technological achievements, a prerequisite for a new social order. The foundation of a classless society began to be laid out immediately with the Decree on the Nationalization of Land (February 1918) and the Decree on Abolition of Private Property in Cities (October 1918). Before the end of 1920, a general program for the planned industrial development of the Soviet Union was outlined and enthusiastically approved by the Eighth Party Congress (December 22, 1920). The initial step in this development was the State Plan for the Electrification of Russia (Goelro), which required the design and construction of thirty power stations with adjacent new settlements for workers. The congress also stipulated the creation of new industrial centers and the development

81 Thesis project for "The City of the Future." Housing colonies stationed in space as satellites of Earth. 1928. Architect: Georgii Krutikov.

of planning and design standards to improve the quality of urban life.[10]

The expectation that speedy electrification and industrialization would soon make socialism and communism a reality stimulated the imagination of many architects and

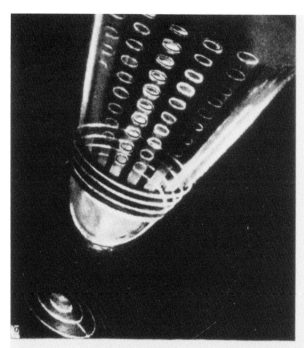

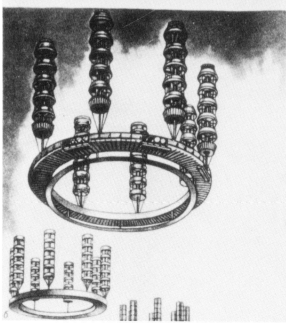

urban designers whose professional training enabled them to project their vision into this future with its ideal social and physical environment. When Soviet technology proved unequal to the task of achieving these visions, Lenin's New Economic Policy (NEP) was introduced. Under NEP, foreign specialists, foreign investments, and the latest scientific and technological achievements were to be brought to the Soviet Union. The initial goal was to create a transitional economic system that would help the Soviet regime retain power until socialist revolutions triumphed in the West. The hopes for an imminent world revolution were shattered by the failure of the Hamburg uprising (Fall 1923), the last revolutionary attempt in Germany. Thereafter, the Soviet government was forced to stabilize itself for an indefinite period of "capitalist encirclement" and to build "socialism in one country."

To end Russia's technical and economic backwardness and "to overtake and outstrip the advanced countries economically and technically,"[1] several policies of importance to architectural development were implemented. First, subscriptions to foreign technical and architectural periodicals were encouraged. Soviet periodicals also frequently reported on foreign technological development. Second, Soviet delegations were sent to leading industrial countries, and Western firms were invited to build major projects in the USSR. Third, technical specialists, among them leading architects, were welcomed to work in the Soviet Union, and by 1930,

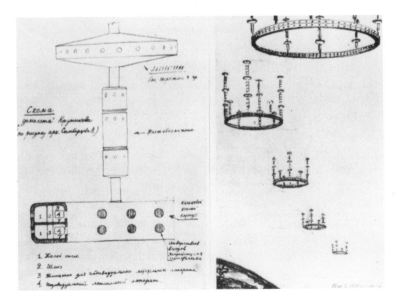

82 Student project "Domoletov" (flying houses). Architects: Georgii Krutikov, V. N. Simbitsev.

some one thousand foreign architects were employed there.[12] Most significantly, Soviet architects were encouraged to design buildings requiring new technologies that were not yet available but soon to be developed.

During the NEP period (1921–28), travel to Western Europe was easier, thus allowing Soviet party leaders, architects, and engineers to learn firsthand about the latest technological achievements. El Lissitzky was sent to Berlin in conjunction with the Russian Art Exhibition at Van Diemen Gallery. While in Germany, he and Ilya Ehrenburg began publishing the periodical *Veshch/Gegenstand/Object*. "The appearance of *Veshch* is an indication that the exchange of objects between young Russian and Western European masters has begun," announced Lissitzky in the first issue. "*Veshch* will study the example of industry, new inventions," he continued, "as immediate material to be used by every conscientious master of

83 Student project "Saturnii." 1928–30. Architect: Viktor Kalmykov.

our time."[13] In 1923, he organized another art exhibition in Berlin and designed the famous Proun Room for it. The Soviet government was presenting to the world a convincing image of political stability, and through art and architectural exhibitions in Germany, Italy, and the United States, creating the impression of a progressive but also stable and tolerant country.[14] Reciprocally, foreign exhibits in Moscow brought projects by such leading modern architects as Walter Gropius, Ludwig Mies van der Rohe, Erich Mendelsohn, Max and Bruno Taut, Max Berg, Ludwig Hilberseimer, and Hugo Haring.[15]

More informative than the exhibitions of foreign architecture were the numerous technical magazines received in Russia. Berlin's *Wasmuth's Monats Hefte,* for example, had six hundred subscribers in the Soviet Union,[16] followed in popularity by *Staedtebau* and *Der Industriebau*. From London the

Russians received the *Architectural Review, The Architect, The Studio;* from Paris, *La Construction moderne, Le Génie civil, L'Architecture,* and *Art et décoration;* and from New York, *American Architect, Architectural Forum, Engineering News Record, Pencil Points,* and others.[17] For those who did not receive foreign magazines, Soviet periodicals regularly reviewed them, translated important articles, and reported on critical developments.

Although Russian architectural periodicals had ceased publication after the revolution, new publications were encouraged after 1922 for the dissemination of information on construction and technology. In 1923, the Moscow Architectural Society (MAO) began publishing its magazine *Arkhitektura.*[18] The same year the State Committee on Construction Affairs of the USSR began publishing its periodical *Stroitelnaia promyshlennost* (Construction industry). The futurist periodical *Lef* and the art journal *Iskusstvo* were also launched in the same year. *Stroitelstvo Moskvy* (Moscow's construction) began the following year, and in 1926 architectural associations such as Asnova and the Society of Contemporary Architects (OSA) began their own publications. Nevertheless, of the 1,291 Soviet periodicals published during 1928, only 4 were dedicated to architecture and construction. The discrepancy between the large number of periodicals for political propaganda, or for scientific and technical information, and the relatively few architectural magazines demonstrates the secondary role allocated to the arts in the Soviet Union. This attitude derives from the Marxist postulate that culture and the arts belong to the superstructure, that is, they are a passive result of the economic system.

The engineers, the scientists, and the inventors were the important professionals, not the artists, and they were eager to learn from capitalist technical expertise. For the structural engineers, books on steel and, above all, concrete structure were translated.[19] The Golden Gate Bridge in San Francisco[20] and American skyscraper construction were analyzed—an extension of the earlier Russian interest described in Chapter 2. Waterways such as the Panama Canal, the canals from the Great Lakes to the Atlantic Ocean, and the Rhine-Danube connection were discussed.[21] Information on aerial photography, especially from Canada and the United States, was also available[22] as was information on flood control and irrigation in the United States, Italy, Germany, and even Palestine.[23] Surprisingly, such narrow publications as the *Bul-*

letins of the Structural Materials Research Laboratory from the Lewis Institute in Chicago and the pamphlets of the British Portland Cement Research Association were also known to Soviet engineers.[24]

Written information was supplemented with frequent visits abroad. In 1924, for example, a Soviet delegation visited workers' settlements in Germany and England.[25] Ebenezer Howard's *Tomorrow: A Peaceful Path to Real Reform* was translated as *Goroda budeshchego* (Cities of the future) in 1904. After Howard's visit to Kharkov in 1912,[26] a Garden City Society was founded in Russia (in 1913) and subsequently exercised considerable influence on pre- and postrevolutionary urban design. In 1925 another influential book on urban design was translated, Camillo Sitte's *City Planning According to Artistic Principles.*[27]

Equally as urgent as the design and construction of workers' settlements was the construction of new industrial plants. Adolf Behne's *Der moderne Zweckbau,* for example, was translated by El Lissitzky from the manuscript and was published almost simultaneously in Germany and Russia. The book discussed and illustrated Albert Kahn's designs for Henry Ford, as well as factories in Germany designed by Peter Behrens, Walter Gropius, and Erich Mendelsohn.[28] Soviet delegations inspected numerous factories in Europe and the United States and invited the best designers to participate in the construction of Soviet industrial enterprises. In 1925 a delegation from Leningrad's Textile Union visited Erich Mendelsohn, surveyed his recently completed hat factory at Lueckenwald and commissioned him to submit designs for the Leningrad Textile Complex including the production process and the required machinery, to provide complete specifications and construction drawings, and to make a competitive bid for procuring the materials from Germany (Figs. 84, 85).[29] The actual construction of this and other projects required importing foreign technology and attracting foreign capital investments. These two goals were to be achieved by "1. granting concessions for construction work; 2. permitting foreign construction firms to open their own offices in the USSR; and 3. allowing foreign investors to benefit from the exploitation of housing structures."[30]

A Soviet delegation from the Economic and Technical Commission toured the United States in 1928–29 and visited Detroit's automobile industry in the spring of 1929. Henry Ford and his talented engineer, Albert Kahn, were already well-known names in the Soviet Union. A contract with

Kahn was signed through Amtorg (the Soviet Trading Corporation in the United States), and the first of an estimated seven hundred industrial plants built by Kahn's firm in Russia was completed within six months. For this plant, the Kahn firm first prepared the plans, and then the steel structure was prefabricated in the United States for delivery to the site in Stalingrad (today's Volgograd). Americans organized and managed the construction as well as the plumbing and electrical installations. Following the successful completion of the first commission, larger and more complex industrial plants were designed and constructed. Albert Kahn was allowed to open an office in Moscow headed by his brother Moritz and staffed with about thirty Americans teaching and training more than fifteen hundred Russians. The contract also stipulated that a group of Soviet engineers would be sent to America "to familiarize themselves with the largest structures and the latest American methods of construction technology."[31] In 1929–30 Kahn's office completed the Stalingrad and Cheliabinsk tractor plants, including the foundries and

84 Leningrad Textile Complex. 1925. Architect: Erich Mendelsohn.

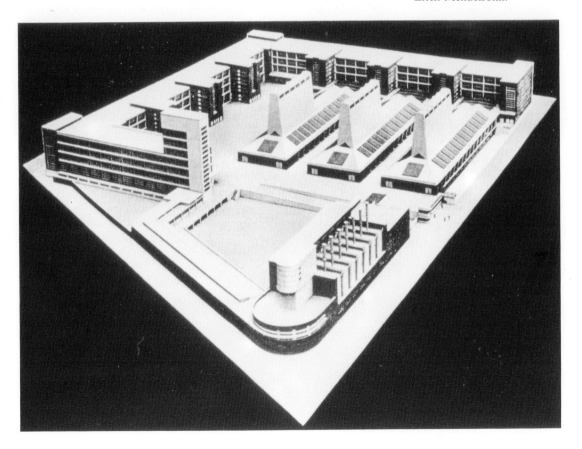

forge shops (Fig. 86). Automobile plants in both Stalingrad and Cheliabinsk followed.[32] The structure, the fenestration, and even wall and roof panels for these industrial buildings were manufactured in America, then shipped and assembled

85   Leningrad Textile Complex. Architect: Erich Mendelsohn.

86   Cheliabinsk Tractor Plant. 1929–30. Architect: Albert Kahn.

on their respective sites in Russia. The necessary tools, equipment, and machinery were all imported from the United
States.

In the spring of 1932, Albert Kahn and twenty-four of his
American employees in Moscow left the Soviet Union (Kahn
departed on March 25, 1932, and his employees followed
within a few weeks).[33] Kahn's departure was attributable to
his failure to reach an agreement with the Soviet government
concerning payment. At the start of 1932, the government
had stopped paying hard currency to foreign workers, offering rubles instead. Nevertheless, because Kahn's office was
required to leave all sets of drawings, specifications, and cal-
culations behind for use in completing projects already un-
derway and for possible future use in additional construction,
the work could be continued by Soviet engineers. Therefore,
whereas about 520 (or 571) of Kahn's industrial plants in the
Soviet Union can be identified,[34] the number of later repe-
titions of his designs is impossible to estimate. Thus, within
three years, one American firm had succeeded in transferring
to the Soviet Union the technological capabilities necessary
for building a socialist utopia.

The majority of foreign architects and engineers working
in the Soviet Union, however, were Germans. Some were
hired as consultants, as for example, the noted German engineer N. Kellen employed in 1928 by the High Council for
State Economy (VSNKh) to organize a bureau of permanent
foreign consultants to advise this most powerful Soviet council. This bureau of foreigners consisted of a twelve-member
high central consulting office, which employed several experienced foreign engineers and sent them to each major construction firm to consult during design and construction. The
bureau was also to bring to construction sites experienced
technical personnel to organize and supervise the construction
process.[35] The German engineers on this bureau were to organize several new research institutes for testing construction
materials and to bring in German construction firms to build
large projects. In 1926 the German firm of P. Kossel und
Sohn A.G. had built housing in Moscow using prefabricated
concrete panels. After these panels, which had been imported
from Germany, had been successfully tested, this firm was
contracted to build several Soviet plants for the prefabrication
of concrete, wood, and glass panels.[36] The best-known building constructed by Kossel is that of Rusgerstroi, the Russo-
German construction firm, in Moscow.[37]

Although experienced engineers were most valuable for

the development of Soviet industry, experienced German architects were also invited as consultants. Bruno Taut, who had built several housing estates around Berlin, had served as a consultant to the Moscow City Soviet since 1926[38] before moving permanently to Moscow in 1932. Taut believed that the new architecture could flourish only in the Soviet Union. "Soviet periodicals follow the latest development of architecture abroad," he noted. Yet, Soviet architects, "assuming that Western architecture has already created the new style, are surprised to learn that there is no such architecture in Germany."[39] The proletariat speaks simply and clearly, Taut asserted. The proletarian regime is clear and unified, and the "new architecture has to be logical, clearly formed, and laconic."[40] Ironically, Taut settled in Moscow as the modern movement in architecture was on the wane.

Many German avant-garde architects shared Taut's conviction about a great future for the modern movement in Soviet Russia. In conjunction with the large 1927 exhibition Contemporary Architecture in Moscow,[41] many students and faculty of Vkhutemas visited Germany while foreign architects visited Russia. The following summer (1928) a group of Bauhaus students visited Moscow.[42] The relationship with the Bauhaus had been close ever since Vasilii Kandinskii left Russia at the end of 1921 to join the Bauhaus faculty. Although architecture was not part of the Bauhaus curriculum until the Swiss architect Hannes Meyer replaced Walter Gropius in 1928, the school had for years designed for industrial mass production and had a record of relating education to technology. Dismissed in August 1930 as director of the Bauhaus, Hannes Meyer and seven radical students formed a Rotfront Brigade and left for the Soviet Union.[43] After the Bauhaus was closed, more students joined their friends in Russia.

The chief architect of Frankfurt-am-Main, Ernst May, made several visits to the Soviet Union and subsequently left for Moscow on May 8, 1930, with a large team mostly from his Frankfurt staff. Among them were experienced architects such as the Swiss-born Hans Schmidt, the Dutchman Mart Stam, Gustav Hassenpflug, who collaborated with Moisei Ginzburg on the Palace of Soviets competition, Walter Schütte, and Grete Schütte-Lihotzky from Vienna.[44] May's Brigade worked on large workers' settlements, the best known being the new industrial town of Magnitogorsk. Though many settlements designed by the foreign architects are known,[45] the importance of their contribution was not in particularizing the planning scheme or individualizing the buildings, but in designing buildings that could be repeated in any place and at any time. A typical neighborhood, for example, consisted of free-standing walk-up apartments (two to four stories high) surrounding an open space with a kindergarten or primary school in the middle. Grete Schütte-Lihotzky was in charge of designing everything children needed, from day-care centers and schools to the furnishings and furniture for children. All her designs were to be mass-produced; the buildings were to be standardized for prefabrication and ease of assembly. When foreign architects were asked to leave the country in 1936, just before the end of the second Five-Year Plan (1933–37), all their work, designs, drawings, and specifications remained as Soviet property. None of them know how many times their projects were repeated throughout the vast Soviet territory.[46]

No mention was made of foreign investment (capital, labor, expertise) when the Soviet regime proudly recounted its achievements in industrializing the country during the first and second Five-Year Plans. The number of people employed in industry, including building, increased almost threefold: from 4.3 million in 1928 to 11.6 million in 1937. Capital investment in industry rose even faster, whereas personal consumption per person declined continuously after 1928, "and did not regain the 1928 level until well after the Second World War."[47] To minimize the importance of foreign help, a fierce attack against the foreigners working in Russia was launched in 1937, a year after most of them had left. The signal for architects was given by V. Molotov in 1937 at the First Congress of Soviet Architects and was immediately followed by sharp criticism in the pages of the architectural press.[48] Soviet architects and engineers had resented the foreigners from the beginning, because of their "patronizing tone in dealing with their Soviet colleagues,"[49] their arrogance and, as El Lissitzky put it, because "even today the foreigners treat us as residents of the western part of Asia, rather than the eastern part of Europe."[50]

Not only Lissitzky but all avant-garde architects in the Soviet Union rightfully claimed to be ahead of the rest of the world in their theoretical and conceptual design development. They were the first to transform art and architectural education and to develop new curricula for the leading art and architecture school Svomas/Vkhutemas/Vkhutein. Ever since the Institute of Artistic Culture (InKhuk) was founded in 1920, they had discussed and often passionately argued about new approaches to design. And they had worked on experimental projects with unprecedented programs. These were not utopias but buildable proposals whose structural feasibility had been calculated, sometimes by foreign engineers. The supporting structure of El Lissitzky's Moscow skyscraper (1924) was designed with the help of the Zurich architect Emil Roth,[51] and Ivan Leonidov's Lenin Library project had its structure checked by Soviet engineers. Numerous avant-garde designs were built during the 1920s, though when their complexity exceeded Soviet technological capabilities, they were built by foreign firms. The first planetarium in Moscow, designed by Vkhutemas graduates Mikhail Barshch and Mikhail Siniavskii in 1927, was built by the German firm of Dyckerhof and Widman (see Chapter 4).[52]

Imaginative urban design proposals, though vastly different from the accepted Western trends, were worked out in detail by Soviet architects. For the new industrial town Avtostroi near Gorkii (Fig. 87), where Kahn's office was building an automobile factory, the Association of Architects-Urbanists (ARU) proposed a most imaginative linear scheme

87 Nizhni-Novgorod (Gorkii) Automobile Plant and Worker's City. 1929. Engineers: The Austin Company, Cleveland, Ohio.

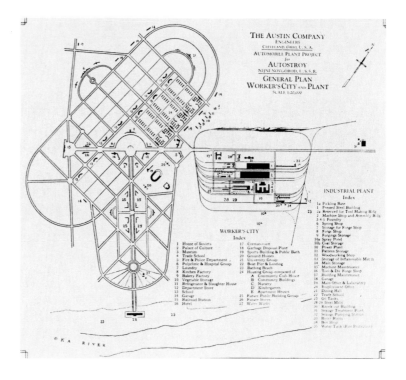

of development. Their 1929 competition entry for this model socialist town of fifty thousand workers was widely publicized not only in Russia but also abroad (Figs. 88, 89). In 1930 it was exhibited at the Monza-Milan International Exposition of Decorative Art and at the Amsterdam International Exhibition of Contemporary Art.[53]

The most publicized and widely discussed competition of 1929 concerned the Green City Resort near Moscow. Although the program required only housing with recreational

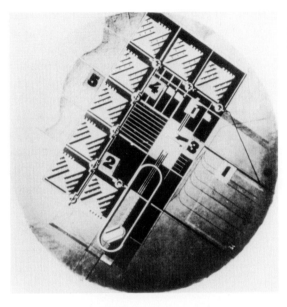

88 ARU project for Avtostroi, near Gorkii. 1929.

89 ARU project for Avtostroi. 1929.

and cultural facilities for one hundred thousand vacationing workers from Moscow, on a site some fifty kilometers from the city, the competition afforded avant-garde architects the opportunity to illustrate their ideal of a permanent socialist town. The project that deservingly won first prize, Ladovskii's carefully conceived proposal, demonstrated what implications the latest technological achievements had for urban design. Praised by the jury as a "socialist garden city," Ladovskii's plan was recommended for implementation. By juxtaposing a pedestrian network with a transportation system of primary arteries and secondary loops to neighborhoods, Ladovskii created an urban system capable of unhindered growth yet complete at each stage of development (Fig. 90). The housing units varied in size, form, and construction methods. Completely prefabricated and furnished cottages were designed to ensure speedy installation and minimal destruction of the site (Figs. 91, 92). Ladovskii patented the cottage structures, but only a few of them were actually erected on the site before experimentation was abandoned in Russia.[54] This decision was most unfortunate for the com-

90 Competition project for Green City, near Moscow. 1929. Architect: Nikolai Ladovskii.

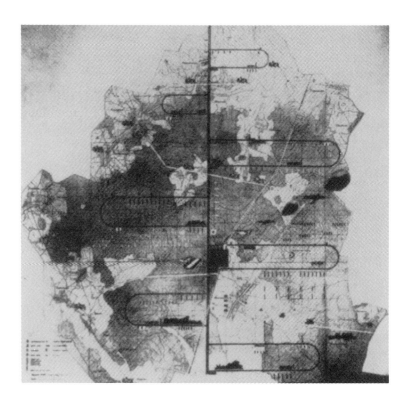

pletion of the project, because for the second stage of housing Ladovskii envisioned using

the highest level of construction technology and industrial standardization with implications for the entire construction industry. . . . If our builders open their eyes to the most advanced technology, the so-called movable structures, . . . we are convinced that . . . housing units could be manufactured perfectly well in the Avtostroi factory and easily transported to the construction site. . . . This could also solve the problem of high-rise construction. . . . The structural skeleton could be erected first on the site. . . . Completely assembled rooms could be lifted into place using cranes and could thus be included in any kind of [building] system.[55]

91   Project plan for Green City. 1929. Architect: Nikolai Ladovskii.

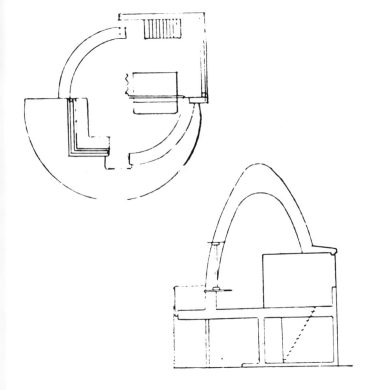

163

A similar construction system was proposed by Le Corbusier almost twenty years later for Marseille and forty years later by Moshe Safdie for Montreal.

The project for the same competition by the rival organization, the Association of Contemporary Architects (OSA) was intended as a model for the reconstruction of Moscow and its transformation to a Green City (Fig. 93). The authors, Moisei Ginzburg and Mikhail Barshch, asserted that contemporary cities, plagued by noise and congestion, were unfit for a healthy life. Lack of fresh air and sunshine necessitated the construction of resorts:

When a man is sick, he is given medicine, but prevention is better than cure. . . . When a city is in bad shape . . . noise, dust, lack of light, air, sun, etc., . . . it is necessary to administer medicine: a

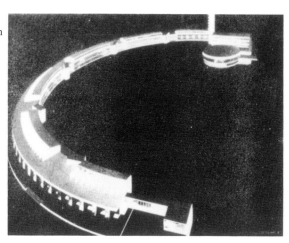

92 Project for Green City, main hotel complex. 1930. Architect: Nikolai Ladovskii.

summer cottage, a health resort, a vacation in a *green city*. This is the medicine. . . . This dual system of poison and antidote is precisely the capitalist system of contradiction. It should be compared with the socialist system—prophylactics, a system requiring the destruction of the city . . . and the resettlement of mankind in a way that solves the problem of labor, rest, and culture as a single continuous process of socialist living.[56]

For this reason, the authors developed their project as a regional plan designed to redistribute Moscow's population. Employment was provided in natural resource exploitation, industries, housing prefabrication, research institutes, and agriculture (Fig. 94). Prefabricated housing units raised on stilts for privacy and an unobstructed view, also provided covered walkways on the ground when arranged in continuous ribbons. Each unit, glazed

entirely front and back "looks spacious and close to nature.... The window-walls could fold and the housing unit
be transformed into a covered terrace surrounded by green-
ery." (Fig. 95).[57] The idea of housing units was further developed in the Section for Population Resettlement where
Moisei Ginzburg headed the architectural group. Established
in 1929 by the State Planning Commission of the USSR, this
section was charged with finding solutions to the pressing
problems of urbanization caused by the speedy industrialization promoted by the first Five-Year Plan. Later Five-Year
Plans were to propel the country toward communism, thus
demanding from the outset a national conceptual framework
for future development.

Stalin's program for maximizing industrial growth was
presented at the Plenum of the Central Committee of the
Communist Party (November 19, 1928) in a speech entitled,
"Industrialization of the Country and the Right Deviation in
the CPSU":

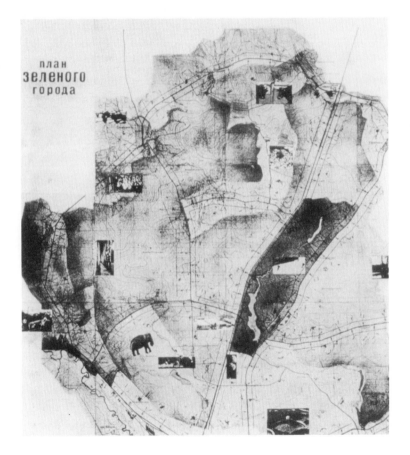

93   Project plan for Green
City. 1929. Architects:
Moisei Ginzburg, Mikhail
Barshch.

Our theses proceed from the premise that a fast rate of development of industry in general, and of the means of production in particular, is the underlying principle of, and the key to, the transformation of our entire national economy along the lines of socialist development. . . .

We have assumed power in a country whose technical equipment is terribly backward. . . . At the same time we have around us a number of capitalist countries whose industrial technique is far more developed and up-to-date than that of our country. Look at the capitalist countries and you will see that their technology is not only advancing, but advancing by leaps and bounds. . . . We must put an end to our technical and economic backwardness. We must do so without fail if we really want to overtake and outstrip the advanced capitalist countries. And only we, Bolsheviks, can do it. But precisely in order to accomplish this task, we must systematically achieve a fast rate of development of our industry.[58]

Stalin's speech provided the impetus for a nationwide discussion on regional development, on the form and shape of socialist settlements, and on the new socialist way of life. The most innovative and radical theory to emerge from this discussion was a theory of decentralization, whereby industry and population were to be evenly distributed over the entire Soviet territory. But this decentralization would depend on maintaining an up-to-date infrastructure (transportation and communication networks and power and water supplies, for example) and on advanced construction technology, standardization, and pre-

94 Project for Green City. 1929. Architects: Moisei Ginzburg, Mikhail Barshch.

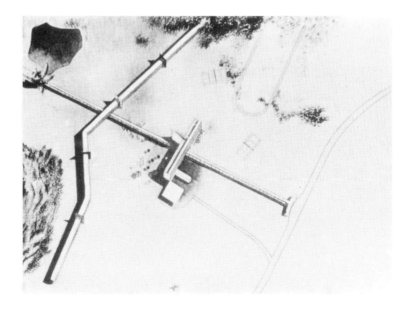

fabrication. Within the Construction Committee (Stroikom) of the RSFSR, a Section for Standardization was founded in mid-1928 and headed by Moisei Ginzburg.[59] The following year, Ginzburg was chosen to head the Section for Population Resettlement, and he brought

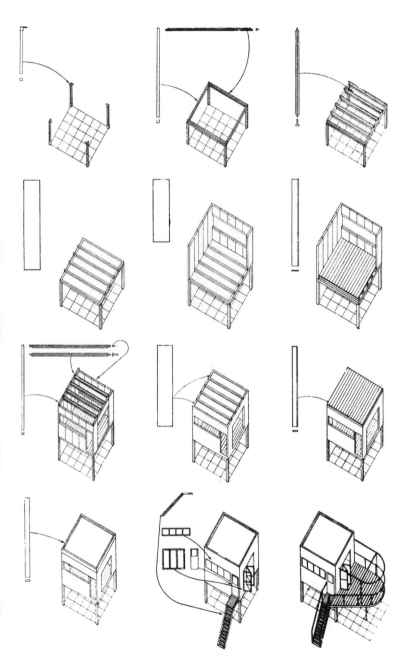

95 Project for Green City, one-room modules. 1929. Architects: Moisei Ginzburg, Mikhail Barshch.

with him many OSA members from the Section of Standardization.[60] The Section for Population Resettlement developed sixty-one standardized units for the Green City site, thirteen of which were approved for prefabrication and experimental construction. The responsibility for this construction was entrusted to a Brigade for Socialist Resettlement within the shareholding company Green City.[61] Construction had just begun in 1931 when a change of attitude toward the avant-garde halted further development.[62]

Today it may seem incredible that a fast-moving car, a large crane, or new machines could generate such enormous excitement, stir the imagination, and make utopias believable. But if one looks carefully at the context within which new high-rise apartments were erected and notices the amazement a concrete mixing truck produced, or the awe a paving

96 Concrete mixer, Moscow. 1930.

168

machine generated in Russia, it is possible to understand the miraculous influence of technology on the human spirit (Fig. 96). For the Russian factory worker, the new spinning machines in the textile factory were probably as fabulous as any fairy tale. For the construction worker, cranes and slip-form construction without the traditional scaffolding must have been dumbfounding (Fig. 97). Public laundries with washing machines and "mechanized ironing machines where eight

97 Slip-form construction of a village water tower. Early 1930s.

people could wash and iron twelve hundred kilos of laundry"[63] or a woman driving an asphalt-rolling machine were inconceivable technological miracles for the man on the street (Figs. 98, 99, 100). How could anyone doubt that utopia had begun to be realized with the first Five-Year Plan? And those who had doubts quipped: "If we cannot build socialism ourselves, we can ask the Western countries to build it for us." In Gorbachev's era this barb seems more pertinent than ever before.

98 Asphalt-rolling ma-
chine. Moscow. 1930.

99 Mechanized public
laundry. Ivanovo. 1930s.

1. B. A. [Boris Arvatov], "Oveshchestvlennaia Utopiia," *Lef,* 1923, no. 1:61–64. In this article, Arvatov, a member of the Proletkult and founder of the periodical *Lef,* promoted Anton Lavinskii's 1922 urban scheme for housing on springs.

2. B. Lunin, ed., *Goroda sotsializma i sotsialisticheskaia reconstruktsiia byta* (Moscow: Rabotnik prosveshcheniia, 1930), 3.

3. M. Ilyn, *The Story of the Five-Year Plan* (Moscow: Cooperative Publishing Society of Foreign Workers in the USSR, 1932), 136–37, 155–56.

4. Darko Suvin, *Other Worlds, Other Seas: Science Fiction Stories from Socialist Countries* (New York: Random House, 1970), xxiii.

5. Earlier literary utopias were rationalized folklore fantasies or mirrored the existing social order, as for example, Vladimir F. Odoevskii's *The Year 4338: Letters from Petersburg* (1835).

6. Alexander Bogdanov, a populist turned Marxist and a member of the Bolshevik Party since 1902, was the founder of the Proletarian Culture and Science Organization, the Proletkult. Following the revolution, this organization grew to include more than eight hundred unions, with fifteen periodicals touting Bogdanov's ideas. Bogdanov planned a third novel to complete his Martian trilogy. He outlined this novel in the poem "A Martian Stranded on Earth" (1924) but never found time to complete it.

7. Alexander Bogdanov, *Red Star: A Utopia,* trans. Charles Rougle (Bloomington: Indiana University Press, 1984), 77.

8. L. M. Sabsovich, *Goroda budushchego i organizatsiia sotsialisticheskogo byta* (Moscow: Gosudarstvennoe tekhnicheskoe izdatelstvo, 1929).

100 Mechanized ironing in public laundry. Moscow. Early 1930s.

Sabsovich, an economist and social scientist, was a member of both Gosplan's Commission on a General Plan and the All-Union Association of Workers in Science and Technology Assisting in the Socialist Reconstruction (VARNITSO). Among Sabsovich's numerous publications, the single most complete source describing his urban design theory is *Sotsialisticheskie goroda* (Moscow: Moskovskii Rabochii, 1930).

9. Tsiolkovskii's earlier works of science fiction—*On the Moon* (1887) and *Daydreams of Earth and Heavens* (1894), which deal with weightless life on the moon and on asteroids—were also republished after the revolution.

10. The architecture of some of these power stations is illustrated in A. Kovalev, "GOELRO i arkhitekture energeticheskikh sooruzhenii," *Arkhitektura SSSR*, 1970, no. 4:40–45; dams and electrical equipment plants are discussed in Antony C. Sutton, *Western Technology and Soviet Economic Development 1917–1930* (Stanford: Hoover Institution Publications, 1968), 185–208. Western technical assistance during the 1930s is the subject of vol. 2 (1971), 177–94.

11. Lenin, *The Impending Catastrophe and How to Combat It*, pamphlet of 1917, as quoted by Stalin in "Industrialization of the Country and the Right Deviation in the CPSU," *Works* (Moscow: Foreign Language Publishing House, 1964), 11:256–66.

12. Kurt Junghanns, "Deutsche Architekten in der Soviet Union während der erste Fünfjahrplan und des Vaterländischen Krieges," *Wissenschaftliche Zeitschrift der Hochschule für Architektur und Bauwesen* (Weimar) 29, no. 2 (1983).

13. *Veshch/Gegenstand/Object* (Berlin), 1922, no. 1–2:1–4.

14. Soviet architecture was exhibited in Hanover, Germany, in 1921 and 1923; Amsterdam in 1923; Venice in 1924; Milan in 1927, 1930, and 1933; Paris in 1925; Salonika, Greece, in 1927; New York in 1926, 1927, 1928, and 1929.

15. *Stroitel'naia promyshlennost'*, 1924, no. 11:736–38.

16. A. I. Dimitriev, "Inostrannye arkhitekturnye zhurnaly," *Stroitel'naia promyshlennost'*, 1926, no. 10:738–39.

17. Ibid., 739.

18. Publication was seized the following year, probably because of MAO's conservative attitude toward the modern movement.

19. For example, K. Kersten's *Concrete Structures*, E. Paton's *Steel Bridges*, A. Jackson's *Contemporary Wood Construction*, among others. See book reviews in *Stroitel'naia promyshlennost'* and *Stroitel'stvo Moskvy*.

20. *Stroitel'naia promyshlennost'*, 1925, no. 3:216.

21. Ibid., 299–372, and *Stroitel'naia promyshlennost'*, 1923, no. 4:42–44.

22. *Stroitel'naia promyshlennost'*, 1925, no. 3:314–18.

23. *Stroitel'naia promyshlennost'*, 1923, no. 1:43–46.

24. These of 1922 were reviewed in *Stroitel'naia promyshlennost'*, 1923, no. 4:48.

25. Reported in *Stroitel'stvo Moskvy*, 1925, no. 1:4.

26. Waclaw Ostrowski, *Contemporary Town Planning: From the Origins to the Athens Chapter* (The Hague: International Federation for Housing and Planning, 1970), 39.

27. This translation is discussed in A. V. Shchusev, "O knige K. Zitte," *Stroitel'stvo Moskvy*, 1925, no. 12:39.

28. "Sovremennaia tselesoobraznaia arkhitektura," *Stroitel'naia promysh-*

lennost', 1925, no. 12:871–73 and El Lissitzky, "Arkhitektura zheleznio i zhelezobetonnoi ramy," *Stroitel'naia promyshlennost'*, 1926, no. 2:59–63.

29. "Erich Mendelsohn's Letter," *Sovremennaia arkhitektura*, 1927, no. 3:108. In this letter, Mendelsohn describes the work he had presented, his business meetings in Leningrad (October 1925, May 1926, July 1926) and complaints about his mistreatment by Soviet engineers.

30. M. Iapol'skii "Inostrannye firmy i stroitel'stvo SSSR," *Stroitel'naia promyshlennost'*, 1926, no. 6–7:410–12.

31. *Stroitel'stvo Moskvy*, 1929, no. 11:40. Kahn's work in Russia is briefly described in Sutton, *Western Technology and Soviet Economic Development* 2:249–52.

32. In the 1936 list, "Industrial and Commercial Building," prepared by A. Kahn, Inc., the following Soviet plants are named: airplane parts and accessories: Kramatorsk and Tomsk; automobile plants: Cheliabinsk, Moscow, Stalingrad, Gorki, Samara; forge shops: Cheliabinsk, Dnepropetrovsk, Kharkov, Koloma, Lubertsk, Magnitogorsk, Nignii Tagil, Stalingrad; machinery and machine tools: Kaluga, Novosibirsk, Upper Solda; roller bearing: Moscow; foundries: Cheliabinsk, Dnepropetrovsk, Kharkov, Koloma, Lubertsk, Magnitogorsk, Sormovo, Stalingrad; machine shops: Cheliabinsk, Lubertsk, Podolsk, Stalingrad, Sverdlovsk; power plants: Yakutsk; steel plants and rolling mills: Kamenskoi, Koloma, Kuznetsk, Magnitogorsk, Nignii Tagil, Sormovo, Upper Tagil; tractor plants: Cheliabinsk, Kharkov, Stalingrad, Tomsk; Leningrad aluminum plant; Ural asbestos plant, etc.

33. Walter Duranty (Moscow correspondent), *New York Times*, 26 March 1932.

34. Anatole Kopp, "Foreign Architects in the Soviet Union during the Two First Five-Year Plans" (Colloquium paper delivered at the Kennan Institute for Advanced Russian Studies, 14 May 1987). (For the expanded text of this presentation, see Chapter 6.)

35. Dr. Ing. N. Keller, "Voprosy inostrannoi technicheskoi pomoshchi," *Stroitel'naia promyshlennost'*, 1929, no. 2:174–76.

36. Arch. M. Markovnikov, "Predstoiashchee v Moskve stroitel'stvo po sisteme 'Kossel,' " *Stroitel'naia promyshlennost'*, 1926, no. 8:553–55; Ing. P. Mikhailov, "Stroitel'stvo 'Rusgerstroiia,' " *Stroitel'naia promyshlennost'*, 1927, no. 2:106–7, and 1927, no. 3:186–88.

37. Mikhailov, "Stroitel'stvo 'Rusgerstroiia,' " no. 3:188. The concession between Tsentrozhilsoiuz (The Central Union of Dwelling Cooperatives) and Kossel was intended to last twenty-five years, but Kossel was ejected in 1928. See Sutton, *Western Technology and Soviet Economic Development* 1:236.

38. Bruno Taut, "Novaia arkhitektura v SSSR," *Stroitel'naia promyshlennost'*, 1926, no. 8:562–64.

39. Ibid., 563.

40. Bruno Taut, "Arkhitektura kak vyrazitel' vlasti," *Stroitel'naia promyshlennost'*, 1926, no. 6–7:465.

41. The exhibition, organized by OSA for Glavnauka is discussed in *Stroitel'stvo Moskvy*, 1927, no. 7:8–11; and in *Stroitel'naia promyshlennost'*, 1927, no. 6–7:450–54.

42. This exchange is briefly mentioned in Arieh Sharon, *Kibbutz and*

Bauhaus: An Architect's Way in a New Land (Stuttgart: Karl Kroemer Verlag, 1976), 30. See also D. Aranovich, "Bauhaus-Dessau," *Stroitel'naia promyshlennost'*, 1928, no. 10:740–44.

43. The members of the Rotfront Brigade were Rene Mensch, Klaus Meimann, Konrad Peuschel, Philipp Teolziner, Bela Scheffler, Anton Urban, and Tibor Weiner.

44. Other known members of the group were Hans Burkhart, Mr. Fritsche, Max Fruhof, Wilhelm Hauss, Werner Hedebrand, Mr. Keil, S. Kolpenetzky, Walter Kratz, Karl Lehmann, Hans Leistikow, Albert Locher, Erich Mauthner, Mr. Niemeyer, Walter Schulz, Walter Schwagenscheidt, and Albert Winter. Eugen Kaufman and Kurt Liebknecht joined the group in 1931. Others joined later—the Hungarian, Fred Forbat; J. W. Lehr; and the chief architect of Cologne, Kurt Meyers, to name a few. The curator of the Vienna Museum for Economics and Trade, Dr. Neurath arrived in Moscow in 1930 with a group of skilled workers and artists to establish the Isostat Institute for Art-in-Statistics. The institute adopted Dr. Neurath's method of creating diagrams by means of symbolic signs. See Sophie Lissitzky-Kuepper, *El Lissitzky* (Boston: New York Graphic Society, 1968), 95.

45. Ernst May's group designed housing estates for numerous cities including Kuznetsk, Orsk, Prokopievsk, Nijnii Tagil, Leninakan, Makaevka, Shcheglovsk, Khibinogorsk. See Christian Borngraeber, "Hans Schmidt and Hannes Meyer in Moskau," *Werk-Archithese*, 23–24 (1978): 37–40.

46. Grete Schütte-Lihotzky in conversation with this author.

47. *The Cambridge Encyclopedia of Russia and the Soviet Union* (Cambridge: Cambridge University Press, 1982), 333. A list of foreign concessions in the Soviet Union for the period 1920–30 is published in Sutton, *Western Technology and Soviet Economic Development* 1:353–63. A list of "Technical-Assistance Agreements Between the Soviet Union and Western Companies, 1929–45" can also be found there (2:363–72).

48. See, for example, A. Mustakov, "Bezobraznoe nasledstvo arkhitektura E. Maja," *Arkhitektura SSSR*, 1937, no. 9:62.

49. Redaktsia, "Voprosy industrannoi tekhnicheskoi pomoshchi," *Stroitel'naia promyshlennost'*, 1929, no. 2:177.

50. Professor El Lissitzky, "Idoly i idolopoklonniki," *Stroitel'naia promyshlennost'*, 1928, no. 11–12:854.

51. H. M. "Po povodu No. 1 'Izvestiia assotsiatisii. novykh arkhitektorov,'" *Stroitel'naia promyshlennost'*, 1926, no. 8:567.

52. M. Barshch and M. Siniavskii, "Planetarii," *SA*, 1929, no. 5:155.

53. G. Krutikov, "K voprosu obshchestveno prostranstvennoi organizatsii poseleniia posledovatelno sotsialisticheskogo tipa. Goroda-Kommuna Avtostroi 1929–1930," *Sovetskaia arkhitektura*, 1931, no. 1–2:29–35.

54. Ladovskii's project is discussed in Ts-on, "K itogam konkursa," *Stroitel'stvo Moskvy*, 1930, no. 6:35–36; "Voprosy planirovki: opyt sotsialisticheskogo goroda sada," *Stroitel'naia promyshlennost'*, 1930, no. 5:450–54; Nikolai Ladovskii, "Goroda otdikha i sotsialisticheskogo byta," *Stroitel'stvo Moskvy*, 1930, no. 3:9–19; and reported to the German readers by Leoni Pilevski, "Neuer Wohnungsbau in der Sowjetunion," *Die Form*, 1931, no. 39:102.

55. Ladovskii, "Goroda otdikha i sotsialisticheskogo byta," 9–13.

56. M. Barshch and M. Ginzburg, "Zelenyi gorod: Sotsialisticheskaia rekonstruktsiia Moskvy," *Sovetskaia arkhitektura*, 1930, no. 1–2:17. The argument in favor of deurbanization is discussed at length in Anatole Kopp, *Town and Revolution: Soviet Architecture and City Planning 1917–1935* (London: Thames and Hudson, 1970), 178–84.

57. Barshch and Ginzburg, "Zelenyi gorod," 31.

58. Joseph Stalin, *Works* (Moscow: Foreign Language Publishing House, 1964), 11:256–66. Reprinted in Morris Bornstein and Daniel R. Rusfeld, eds., *The Soviet Economy: A Book of Readings* (Homewood, Ill.: 1970), 17–23.

59. The section was staffed by members of OSA: M. O. Barshch, V. N. Vladimirov, A. L. Pasternak, and G. R. Sum-Shik.

60. K. N. Afanasev, M. O. Barshch, V. N. Vladimirov, G. A. Zunblat, I. F. Milinis, S. V. Orlovskii, G. G. Savinov, and N. B. Sokolov.

61. The membership of the brigade, organized on October 4, 1930, consisted of almost the same OSA members as the architectural group of the Section for Population Resettlement. See the announcement of the brigade's organization in *SA*, 1930, no. 6:17.

62. The units are discussed and illustrated in S. O. Kahn-Magomedov, *M. Ia. Ginzburg* (Moscow: Stroiizdat, 1972), 114–29.

63. Gosplan SSSR, *Rekonstruktsiia gorodov SSSR* (Moscow: Gosudarstvennoe izdatelstvo "Standartizatsiia i Ratsionalizatsiia," 1933), n.p.

6 FOREIGN ARCHITECTS IN THE SOVIET UNION DURING THE FIRST TWO FIVE-YEAR PLANS

Anatole Kopp

SOVIET architecture of the 1920s—avant-garde architecture—was largely unresearched in the West until the mid-1960s.* Since then, in Europe, in the United States, and also progressively in the Soviet Union, various studies have been devoted to this subject. What has remained largely unexamined, however, is the activity of a large number of foreign technicians who went to work in the USSR beginning in 1928. Their participation in various construction projects and in the development of Soviet architecture is the subject of this chapter.

---

* Because of the extremely small number of studies on this subject by Soviet specialists, research has been rather difficult, and an explanation of sources might be useful. In part, this study is based on interviews with architects who worked in the Soviet Union in the late 1920s and early 1930s, including Hans Blumenfeld, a former German, later of Toronto; Grete Schütte-Lihotzky of Vienna; Konrad Püschel of Weimar; Charlotte Perrland of Paris, who worked with Le Corbusier (Charles-Eduard Jeanneret) on various projects, in particular the Tsentrosoiuz building in Moscow; Gustav Hassenpflug; the widow of the German-Swiss architect Hannes Meyer; and the French architect André Lurcat, who worked in the USSR from 1934 until 1937. Articles were published in Soviet professional journals discussing foreign architects—in particular, André Lurcat and Le Corbusier—but most concerned the work of these architects prior to their departure for the Soviet Union. The German-language weekly *Moskauer Rundschau* devoted some space to the activity of foreign specialists and to lectures held at the Moscow Club for Foreign Technicians, which during the mid-1930s counted several thousand members. Articles by foreign architects can also be found in Soviet publications, but these were rarely about their opinions of Soviet architecture. Journals published by friendship societies with ties to the USSR, such as the German *Neues Russland,* offered a vehicle for several preeminent German architects to express their views about their work in the USSR. In addition, the Bauhaus colloquia provided a forum for discussing German-Soviet relations in the field of architecture and design. Finally, various German architectural historians, such as Christian Borngräber of West Berlin, and Kurt Junghanns from the Humboldt University in West Berlin, have studied foreign participation in the development of Soviet architecture, and a recent article by Carmen Karin Jung and Dietrich Worbs in the German *Bauwelt* provides information on May's activity in the USSR. Other sources included Le Corbusier's writings and archival material at the construction firm Albert Kahn of Detroit, Michigan.

The importance of the presence of foreign—particularly German—architects in the Soviet Union is stressed in a study by Kurt Junghanns. According to Junghanns, "the Section of Foreign Architects within the Union of Soviet Architects [Obshchestvo sovetskikh arkhitektorov] between 1933 and 1936 comprised between 800 and 1,000 members despite the fact that not every foreign architect was a member [of the Union]. It is characteristic that about half of them were Germans."[1]

Although the mass emigration of architects remained a purely German phenomenon, other European architects emigrated during the 1930s for generally the same reasons as their German colleagues. The first reason that comes to mind for this emigration is the economic depression that began in the United States in 1929 and reached Germany in the 1930s. By 1932, 45 percent of the active population in Germany was out of work, and the creation of social housing projects—one of the most successful achievements of the Weimar Republic—had practically come to a standstill. But the economic depression alone does not explain why the mass emigration was confined to German architects. After all, the economic crisis in Great Britain was almost as bad as that in Germany, yet British architects did not emigrate en masse. Moreover, economic conditions do not explain why such a great number of German architects went to the Soviet Union.

Hitler's rise to power in January 1933 may have been another reason for this emigration. But, although the exact dates on which each individual architect—or groups of architects—emigrated are not known, the "great names" in German architecture left Germany at the beginning of the 1930s. Ernst May and Hannes Meyer left in 1930—that is, before Hitler came to power. Jewish heritage could have been a decisive reason to emigrate, yet few of the architects who actually emigrated to the USSR were Jews. Sources that discuss the emigration of young Jewish architects suggest that most chose to go to Palestine after 1933.[2]

Thus, although economic depression and the rise of Hitler clearly played a role in the emigration of architects to the Soviet Union, these events were not the decisive factors behind this emigration. One such decisive factor concerns the way the USSR was perceived by an important segment of the Western European population, by part of the working class, and also by a sizable number of intellectuals, including architects. In addition, German architects were motivated by their belief in the principles of the modern movement—or *neues Bauen,* as it was called in Germany—as well as by the nature and social structure of their clientele.

PERCEPTIONS OF THE USSR DURING THE 1920S

Much of what is known today about the first decade in the history of the Soviet Union was then unknown outside the USSR. Moreover, the Western democracies were viewed by many in light of the First World War and its consequences, the perceived social injustice in these countries, and the inability of the Western democracies to offer their citizens a worthwhile goal in life. An abundant literature on the subject in Western Europe as well as in America testifies to this sentiment. Soviet Russia seemed to be the country where the ideas of modern architecture were becoming the guiding principles of architecture and town planning. This was reflected not only in professional articles and on drafting boards, but in the architectural landscape as well.[3]

The First International Congress of Modern Architecture (CIAM)[4] took place in 1928 in La Sarraz, Switzerland. The most prestigious avant-garde architects participated in the event, and they adopted a manifesto clearly showing that social, economic, and political considerations were essential components of modern architectural theory—a theory that shared many common principles with those followed by Soviet architects of that period.

The undersigned architects proclaim that their production must express the spirit of our time. . . . Conscious of the profound transformation brought to the social structure by mechanisation, they acknowledge that the transformation of the social order and of the social life lead to a corresponding transformation of architectural phenomena. The precise goal of their encounter is to return architecture to its real basis, which is economic and sociological.[5]

Modern architects in Germany, Austria, Belgium, the Netherlands, and Czechoslovakia had begun to work for a new client: the people. A small group of French avant-garde architects, including Le Corbusier, hoped that the same phenomenon would occur in France. According to the German architect Walter Gropius, "It is not more private villas that must be built, but hundreds of apartments. Not houses for those who are rich in capital, but good houses that can be used by the workers, houses that are not an answer to an aesthetic commission but to objective facts."[6]

The ideas expressed at La Sarraz in 1928 were very close to those expressed by specialists at the time in the Soviet Union. Many architects of the modern movement publicly expressed enthusiasm about what was being done—or what they thought was being done—in the field of Soviet architecture and town planning, and also in the social and political life of the Soviet Union. After his first visit to Moscow in 1928 Le Corbusier wrote: "I found in Moscow people working tirelessly at the invention of a new architecture . . . searching for the most characteristic, the most pure solutions. . . . One feels in Moscow, be this artificial or deeply motivated, the forthcoming signs of a new world."[7]

Furthermore, Le Corbusier compared work opportunities for Soviet architects to work opportunities for architects in the West:

I have lately been observing in Russia the birth of modern architecture. While we have, for the past thirty years, worked endlessly at narrow and humiliating tasks, this country [the Soviet Union] exhorts its architects. It calls on them to achieve [architectural] types, pure organisms . . . new regulations have been adopted. . . . The formless building lots of the West have forced us to practice an orthopedic architecture; the free land of the USSR brings us the free plan. *US:* crippled combinations exhausting a professional knowledge that once upon a time made for the glory of this country; *THEY:* [Architectural] organisms of the period of the reconstruction.[8]

In 1930, Ernst May, chief architect of the city of Frankfurt—a "bourgeois" architect by Soviet standards—went to work in the Soviet Union with a team of architects and technicians. Before his departure he said, "Politics is none of my business. I am a German architect, and I work for the Soviet Government in the hope of being at the same time useful to the German economy."[9] But he also said, "Nobody can predict whether the greatest national experiment of all times is going to succeed. But it is infinitely more important for me to take part in this immense task than to worry about the security of my private existence."[10]

Friendship society publications, such as *Soviet Russia Today, Neues Russland, Russie neuve,* and *L'URSS en construction,* presented a positive and enthusiastic picture of the USSR, especially when compared with the grim picture of the West during the Depression. Both May, who was generally apolitical, and Walter Gropius spoke positively of the USSR in

Neues Russland.[11] Bruno Taut, who designed many of the
social housing complexes in the Berlin region, also viewed
the USSR in a positive light. After visiting Taut's housing
complexes, Anatolii Lunacharskii, the People's Commissar
of Enlightenment, said: "That is built socialism."[12] Taut traveled extensively in the Soviet Union and found support
among Soviet planners for his ideas of urban decentralization,
which were very similar to those defended by a number of
Russian specialists.

For many architects, the West offered only limited projects
and the possibility of unemployment. Russia, on the contrary, was seen as the "birthplace" of modern architecture—
a country where scientific planning governed land development, as opposed to the apparent anarchy that existed among
planners in the West. The innovative approaches to architecture practiced in the USSR contrasted with the sterile Western
approaches that made use of bygone styles and worn-out
techniques. And above all, in the USSR changes were taking
place at an unprecedented speed. To many architects, the
Soviet Union seemed to be the land described by Vladimir
Maiakovskii in *The Building Sites and the Men of Kuznetsk.* In
this land, in four years—the four years of the first Five-Year
Plan (1928–32)—a place of wilderness was to become a
garden-town. Comparisons with the West during the
Depression of the 1930s enhanced this image of the USSR,
where, after the launching of the first Five-Year Plan, unemployment had given way to a shortage of manpower.

GERMAN ARCHITECTS OF THE *NEUES BAUEN*

In Germany, by the end of the 1920s, modern architecture
was no longer considered an experimental activity or artistic
fantasy, as it was in most parts of Europe; it had become a
mass phenomenon. The distinguishing features of modern
architecture were its use of both simplified architectural forms
and techniques that had been adapted to new building materials and its particular clientele. Whereas modern architects
in other European nations during that time were receiving
their commissions from wealthy intellectuals and artists, German architects of the *neues Bauen* worked for municipal authorities, who were usually elected on social democratic platforms, and with labor unions to construct housing
projects—an activity that had been actively pursued by the
German Social Democratic Party since the middle of the nine-

teenth century.[13] By the end of the 1920s, countless *Siedlungen* (housing complexes) had been designed by preeminent architects of the modern movement, such as May, Taut, and Gropius, and built throughout Germany by housing cooperatives. In Frankfurt, May designed approximately eight thousand apartments in four years—as well as schools, kindergartens, and commercial facilities—making use of the most advanced building techniques and modern, though moderate, architectural forms.

Another aim of the modern movement was to define "minimum lodging," or *minimum Wohnungen,* for a working-class family. The concept of minimum lodging was not thought of in purely economic terms. According to May, "We, the architects of *neues Bauen,* are fighting without mercy against such economies. . . . We declare war against the partisans of such an uneconomical economy. We calculate otherwise by putting the well-being of men above all mathematical figures."[14] These architects considered the humanitarian and social aspects of architecture essential to their professional practice.

The architects of the new architecture are united, without distinction of nationality, by their compassion toward men in need; one cannot imagine them without a social consciousness; one can even say that they have firmly decided to make social considerations the first priority of modern architecture. . . . They deny the legitimacy of any housing group that provides satisfying living conditions only to the fortunate elite. They fight for the amelioration of the fate of the poorest of the poor.[15]

Modern German architects' concern for the "poorest of the poor" and their ideas regarding the function of architecture in some ways paralleled similar developments in architectural thought in the USSR. "Function," it was believed, had a broader meaning than was implicit in the term *functionalism.* The main function of architecture was to contribute to social change, to serve as one of the "tools" of the transformation of society.[16] Many German architects believed in Soviet ideology regarding the development of culture, in particular regarding the development of architecture, which was considered to be dependent on the working class:

Today we have neither a church nor autocracy nor feudalism as creators of style. It is neither the cathedral nor the castle that orient construction. The direction [of construction] is now in other hands, in the hands of those who construct the buildings, who produce the building materials, who extract them from the quarries and from the mines. . . . It is the mass of the workers . . . that can today provide the basis for good architecture and no longer divine revelation or the blessings of God.[17]

Similar ideas regarding the role of architecture in society were shared by many modern architects outside the Soviet Union, but, except in Germany, these concepts remained confined to theory. At a preparatory meeting of the Fourth CIAM, the Polish delegation commented:

> Architects must consider political and economic problems to be consequences of their activity. Obviously the social revolution up until now has never been the result of the work of architects; however, architecture is perfectly capable of expressing and personifying radical ideas through construction. The revolutionary principles of the CIAM in the fields of construction, technique, housing, and town planning can therefore exert a direct effect on future forms of life, an effect whose capacity for coercion shall be as powerful as the firing of a gun but much more fruitful.[18]

A shared belief regarding the function of architecture was one of the reasons for the mass migration of architects to the Soviet Union during the 1930s.

SOVIET ARCHITECTURE DURING THE 1920S

For Soviet architects in the 1920s, in particular Soviet constructivist architects, the function of architecture had little to do with its function before the Bolshevik Revolution. The main characteristic of Soviet avant-garde architecture of the 1920s was its proclaimed objective of creating an architectural landscape that would reflect the ideals of the revolution. This correlation between Soviet architecture and social concerns is the main source of interest in the theories, projects, and unique constructions generated by Soviet architecture during the 1920s. This correlation suggests that the architecture of the 1920s was not only an artistic avant-garde movement but also a social and political movement. This thought was expressed by the theoretical spokesman of the constructivists, Moisei Ginzburg, in the constructivists' publication *Sovremennaia arkhitektura* (contemporary architecture):

> One will say that every architect . . . has a goal. . . . But the constructivists give the notion of a goal a precise meaning. . . . The constructivists consider the problem of the goal in relation to all the changes occurring in our way of life that provide the basis for an entirely new conception of housing. The goal for us is not to execute a commission as such, but to work in conjunction with the

proletariat, to participate in the construction of a new life, of a new way of life.[19]

For constructivist architects—and for party and government leaders—architecture became one of the tools of what at the time was called *perestroika byta,* or reconstruction of the way of life. This idea was expressed by M. Okhitovitch, a theoretician of Soviet town and regional planning during the 1920s: "The goal of architecture of our period is not the construction of a given building but the 'Construction,' the shaping of new social relations resulting from new production conditions, under the form of buildings whose common character will be the expression of their social and productive contents."[20] Soviet avant-garde architects began to consider buildings and even entire towns "tools of social changes," or *sotsialnye kondensatory* (social condensers).

During this time, the urbanists and deurbanists were debating the role of the city in the development of Soviet society. The industrialization of the USSR was pursued according to a decentralized rather than a centralized scheme. This meant that most of the great industrial projects of the first Five-Year Plan were located in unpopulated or scarcely populated areas far from towns. Therefore, these projects could not benefit from existing infrastructures, and the surrounding environment had to be built simultaneously with particular industrial projects. Moreover, not all of these sites were originally intended to be towns. In order to design and supervise the building of these towns, technicians, architects, and town planners were needed. But these specialists were scarce in the Soviet Union during the 1920s. In addition, the discussions among Soviet specialists in 1928–29 were extremely theoretical and abstract, focusing on questions such as the nature of the *sotsgorod* (socialist town) and whether or not towns built under capitalism and designed to serve its purposes could be transformed and adapted to the new way of life resulting from *perestroika byta.*

The urbanists favored a decentralized system of human establishments, each not exceeding forty thousand inhabitants; everyday life was to be almost totally collectivized through the construction of commune houses *(doma kommuny),* factory-kitchens *(fabriki-kukhni),* accommodations for children, and other communal arrangements. The deurbanists stood for the elimination of anything resembling a town, large or small. Individual "living cells" were to be erected along main highways; factories were to be placed next to sources of raw materials; territories were to be made equivalent to each other through the even distribution of electric power throughout the entire country; and transportation from residences to production areas was to be provided by automobiles and buses, "as in America." Despite its abstract and often utopian character, this discussion helped establish certain planning principles, although final decisions were postponed until theoretical principles had been clarified. But the Five-Year Plan demanded immediate decisions and could not wait for the end of prolonged deliberations. By inviting foreign specialists—who had not been involved in the 1928–29 discussions—to work in the USSR, Soviet authorities were forced to curtail the debate and to begin applying new principles in town planning.

Thus it was decided to "import" architects into the Soviet Union. In considering which architects to invite, Soviet authorities ruled out architects who were continuing to work in the classical tradition, designing "unique" buildings for prestigious programs, even though these architects represented the majority of the profession at that time.[21] Instead, they sought architects whose projects were suited for mass production and mass housing, who seemed to understand the needs and objectives of the Five-Year Plan, and who advocated designing architecture not for the "happy few," but instead for the masses. In short, they sought architects of the modern movement, and the personal histories of the invited architects and descriptions of their work confirm that the Soviet authorities fulfilled their intent. These architects were looking for work, but in addition they went to the USSR because they thought that their style of architecture met a need; many felt that they were pursuing a mission, that they were contributing to the success of what Ernst May had called "the greatest national experiment of all times."

Of the one thousand architects who, according to Junghanns, worked in the Soviet Union during the early 1930s, not more than fifty names are known; most are names of architects who were well-known before they went to the USSR or architects who, after their return, spoke or wrote about their experiences. Although the majority of these architects—approximately five hundred—were from Germany, others came originally from the Netherlands, Hungary, and Switzerland but worked for a time in Germany before leaving for the USSR. Only two French architects worked in the USSR. The American architects who worked in the Soviet

Union were generally specialists in the field of industrial architecture.

Foreign architects in the USSR can also be classified according to their political opinions. Some were militant Communists, and ideology was a determinant in their decision to emigrate; most were "socially minded," like most members of the modern movement. Some of the foreign architects were the "great" architects of the 1920s and 1930s, whereas others were young architects who were unknown in the 1930s but became important after the war.

GERMAN ARCHITECTS IN THE SOVIET UNION

The first German architect known to have worked in the Soviet Union was Oswald Schneideratus, who emigrated in 1924. His reasons seem to have been purely political; he was a militant Communist in Berlin, and in 1921 he was in charge of a party military organization. His departure to the Soviet Union was a party decision, taken in order to avoid his arrest, although he was also a qualified architect. In the USSR, he became an active professional known for various important projects, including some in the Autonomous Soviet Socialist Republic of the Volga Germans, and he is the only foreign architect mentioned in the 1962 edition of the *History of Soviet Architecture*. Schneideratus died in Moscow in 1937. Werner Schneideratus, Oswald's son, shared his father's opinions. Werner was arrested by the Nazis, but he managed to escape to the Soviet Union, where he found work in the office of the American architect Albert Kahn in Moscow.

Bruno Taut was the chief architect of the two most well-known *Siedlungen,* Berlin-Britz and Onkel Toms Hütte, and he was formerly a member, as was Walter Gropius, of the postwar artistic-revolutionary organization Arbeitsrat für Kunst (Council of the Workers of the Arts). Interested in the Soviet Union, Taut wrote articles for *Neues Russland,* and he traveled to the USSR in 1926. In 1932, he closed his Berlin office and moved to Moscow. Taut lectured about the German building industry, but he obtained few commissions from the Soviets, and none of them was ever built.

Ernst May organized a model municipal planning and building organization in Germany that performed all architectural, planning, and building tasks—from preliminary sketches to the control and direction of construction, from choice of building sites to development plans. Many large building elements were factory produced, and building sites were organized using assembly lines. In the field of town planning, May was one of the promoters of the idea of the *Trabantenstadt*—that is, independent satellite communities designed to limit the growth of towns. This idea, practiced in Frankfurt, pleased Russian planners, who saw the uncontrolled growth of urban centers as one of the evils of capitalism and who advocated decentralization in the discussion between the urbanists and deurbanists. After preliminary trips to the Soviet Union, May moved to Moscow on May 8, 1930, with a team of architects and building technicians composed essentially of his Frankfurt crew.[22] Soviet authorities negotiated an unusual contract with May through the Tsekombank (Central Communal Bank); contracts with foreign technicians were usually negotiated on an individual basis. Soviet authorities intended to use May's Brigade, or *Brigada Maia,* not only as an architectural and town-planning team, but also as a model organization for Soviet planners and builders.

May's Brigade was put in charge of important housing developments for Kuznetsk, Prokopievsk, Nizhnii Tagil, Orsk, Leninakan, Makaevka, Shcheglovsk, Chibinogorsk, and Magnitogorsk—the last being the most important of May's commissions. May and his team were also invited to take part in the competition for the reconstruction of Moscow that was to transform Moscow into an "exemplary socialist city" *(obraztsovyi sotsialisticheskii gorod).* They were also put in charge of a great many housing, school, and clinic projects in various parts of the Soviet Union.

After 1930, many German and German-speaking architects traveled to Moscow in order to join May's Brigade. Among the additions were Fred Forbat, J. W. Lehr, Eugen Kaufmann, and Kurt Liebknecht. May—who described himself as apolitical, despite his general interest in the Soviet Union—lived, as did members of his team, in conditions that bore no comparison with those of his Soviet colleagues. May's team was paid in foreign currency and had access to the special shops reserved for foreigners.

Hannes Meyer, another of the "great" modern architects, appeared to be more overtly political than May. In 1928, Meyer succeeded Gropius as head of the Dessau Bauhaus, where he introduced architecture and planning into the curriculum and opened the Bauhaus to industry and labor organizations. He also incorporated the social sciences into the teaching of architecture; in those days this was not common practice among architectural schools. The "leftist" orientation of the Bauhaus under Meyer undoubtedly led to his dismissal in August 1930, despite the fact that Meyer's Bauhaus had acquired a more contemporary image than the one it displayed during the period following its founding in 1920. The Bauhaus maintained relations with its Russian equivalent, the Moscow Vkhutemas (State Higher Art and Technical Studios), created in 1921. Teaching methods at the Vkhutemas were somewhat similar to the methods of the Bauhaus. And there were exchanges between the two institutions; for example, El Lissitzky (L. M. Lissitsky), a Soviet architect and designer at Vkhutemas, often visited the Dessau institution,[23] and in 1928, a Bauhaus delegation visited the Moscow Vkhutemas.[24]

After his dismissal from the Bauhaus, Meyer traveled to the Soviet Union, where he organized the Rotfront Brigade. The seven Bauhaus architecture students who belonged to the Rotfront Brigade were also members of the Bauhaus communist cell: Philipp Tolziner, Konrad Püschel, Tibor Weiner, Rene Mensch, Bela Scheffler, Klaus Meumann, and Anton Urban. Unlike May, Meyer voiced his political positions. When leaving for Moscow he declared:

After many years of working within the capitalist system, I am convinced that working under such conditions is quite senseless. In view of our Marxist and revolutionary conception of the world, we, the revolutionary architects, are at the mercy of the insoluble contradictions of a world built on animal individualism and the exploitation of man by man.

I am leaving for the USSR to work among people who are forging a true revolutionary culture, who are achieving socialism, and who are living in that form of society for which we have been fighting here under the conditions of capitalism.

I beg our Russian comrades to regard us, my group and myself, not as heartless specialists, claiming all kinds of special privileges, but as fellow workers with comradely views ready to make a gift to socialism and the revolution of all our knowledge, all our strength, and all the experience that we have acquired in the art of building.[25]

In accordance with these principles, the Rotfront Brigade lived and worked in conditions quite different from those of May's Brigade. Although May employed a relatively large number of Soviet workers in his brigade,[26] it was essentially a "foreign" unit; his German workers generally remained isolated from Soviet workers; and his commissions were limited to those passed on by Soviet authorities. By contrast,

Meyer's group was much more integrated into Soviet society. For example, Meyer worked for Giprogor (State Institute of Town Building) and was in charge of development plans for various localities. He was also a member of the commission that developed the design competition for the Palace of Soviets—a politically important institution. He also served on the editorial boards of *Sovetskaia arkhitektura* (Soviet architecture) and *Arkhitektura za rubezhom* (Architecture abroad),[27] both of which—particularly the first—approached architecture from a political point of view.

Hannes Meyer was a devoted propagandist for Soviet architecture and society. He traveled extensively throughout Western Europe, lecturing and writing laudatory articles about the USSR for the international architectural press. As a town planner in the USSR, Meyer designed several important new settlements, such as the one for 240,000 inhabitants in Nizhnii Kurilsk and the one for the Jewish autonomous region, Birobidzhan, for which he is best known. Along with May, Kurt Meyer, and Le Corbusier, he entered the competition for the reconstruction of Moscow in 1932. In addition, Hannes Meyer worked on various other projects, such as a school in Gorkii designed for 16,000 students. Nevertheless, soon after its formation, Meyer's Rotfront Brigade was disbanded, and its members were assigned to different Soviet design organizations; some remained in the Soviet Union until the end of the Second World War.

May and Meyer illustrate the political spectrum along which almost all German architects could be positioned. Special mention, however, must be made of Margarete (Grete) Schütte-Lihotzky, who is possibly the only foreign female architect ever to have worked in the Soviet Union. Austrian by birth, Schütte-Lihotzky joined May's team in Frankfurt in 1926. There she designed what became known as Die Frankfurter Küche (The Frankfurt kitchen), which was intended to exemplify the concept of minimum lodging and to ease women's domestic work through a rational arrangement of component elements. In the Soviet Union, Schütte-Lihotzky was in charge of all architectural planning concerning children—including the design of furniture as well as of buildings and facilities for schools and day-care centers.

It is more difficult to say precisely what work other German architects did in the Soviet Union because most of them worked with Soviet architects in Soviet teams and as members of the large artels created at the beginning of the 1930s. From Junghanns's study, it is known that Hans Schmidt, a

German-Swiss architect, who was close to Meyer in his architectural and political views, designed many housing schemes for the industrial towns of the first and second Five-Year Plans; after the Second World War, he worked in East Germany. Kurt Meyer, the chief architect of Cologne, participated in the competition for the reconstruction of Moscow, but little is known of his other activities. Fred Forbat, a Hungarian architect who worked in Germany in the field of housing, joined May's team in the USSR. Gustav Hassenpflug worked with Moisei Ginzburg on several projects, including an entry in the Palace of Soviets competition. Members of Taut's group included J. Neumann, H. Zucker, Joseph Neufeld, and W. Neuziel. Hans Blumenfeld was employed by various large Soviet architectural firms. Other German architects who worked in the USSR included Heintz Abraham, Marinus Gewin, W. Hämer, W. Hedebrand, Gerhardt Kosel, W. Kratz, Wilhelm Kreis, F. Schumacher, K. Volker, and M. Wagner. The activities of many other German architects in the USSR remain to be discovered.

THE FRENCH ARCHITECTS LE CORBUSIER AND LURCAT

Le Corbusier was probably the most spectacular figure in the modern movement during the 1920s and 1930s. Lurcat was also a well-known figure in contemporary architecture, although his ideas and projects lacked the universal appeal of many of Le Corbusier's productions.

Unlike other foreign architects who lived and worked in the Soviet Union, Le Corbusier never settled in the USSR; his contact with the Soviet Union was limited to a few short stays in Moscow. Nevertheless, the Tsentrosoiuz (the Central Consumers' Union Building), which was Le Corbusier's major Soviet commission, is one of the best-known examples of modern architecture in the Soviet Union, and Le Corbusier was the only foreign architect who could claim that at least one example of his work in the USSR remained relatively unaltered. *The Radiant City,* Le Corbusier's major book on town planning, grew out of a questionnaire sent to foreign architects by the municipal authorities of Moscow, asking, in precise questions, for advice on housing and town planning. Le Corbusier responded to this questionnaire on June 8, 1930, with a detailed answer of sixty-six typewritten pages entitled "Résponse à Moscou." Le Corbusier's final attempt to contribute his own ideas to the development of Soviet architecture was his entry in the competition for the Palace of Soviets—the competition that marked the breaking point in the evolution of Soviet architecture within the international modern movement.

Unlike Le Corbusier, André Lurcat moved to the Soviet Union after his first visit, which lasted six weeks. He was invited to visit the country as a member of the French-Soviet friendship organization in order to assist with the organization's propaganda work. Lurcat's reputation in the Soviet Union was undoubtedly due to the quality of his architecture, particularly his last project, a school in the suburban Parisian town of Villejuif. This project gained attention in the Soviet Union partly because Villejuif was a communist municipality whose mayor was Paul Vaillant-Courturier, a leading figure in the French communist movement. Another factor was the school's name: the Groupe scolaire Karl Marx. Lurcat worked in the USSR for three years as an architect and as a professor at the Vkhutemas. His work in the Soviet Union, which was confined mainly to isolated buildings, shows a constant effort to produce structures in conformity with the evolution of Soviet architectural theories.

THE GROWTH OF SOCIALIST REALISM DURING THE 1930S

The period from the end of the 1920s to the mid-1930s when most foreign architects voluntarily or involuntarily left the USSR was characterized by change in Soviet architectural theory and practice. Prior to 1928–29, constructivism had been the major current of Soviet architecture, but during the 1930s socialist realism gradually became the dominant, and then the only accepted, theory in architecture, as in all areas of culture.

Outside the Soviet Union, few knew about these changes. In May 1930, May's Brigade left Berlin in a "joyous" mood, believing its move to the USSR was made in order to work in the "birthplace" of modern architecture.[28] Coverage of foreign architects in the Soviet architectural press was ideologically oriented, and there was practically no coverage of May's arrival. Even earlier, in an article on Taut's lecture in Moscow on May 25, 1926—when Soviet construction was practically at a standstill—the editorial committee of *Stroitelnaia promyshlennost* (Construction industry) emphasized

Taut's support of the Soviet Union rather than the architectural and technical aspects of his lecture. Regarding the lecture, the journal wrote: "As a conclusion to this review [on Taut's lecture], one can state with certitude that not a single remark made by our Berlin comrade has concerned anything that has not already been said . . . by our builders and architects."[29]

Minimizing the contribution of foreign architects was characteristic of the Soviet press. Moreover, as a rule, at the end of foreigners' stays in the USSR or after their departure, their work would be sternly criticized. When foreign architects arrived in the USSR, the Soviet architectural press would publish articles about the tragic state of architecture in Western Europe and the United States, which it claimed was due to capitalism and the Depression. The Soviet press also published articles by foreign architects; these articles usually either discussed the "objective superiority" of the Soviet approach toward architecture or provided a narrow technical analysis of architecture, town planning, and other subjects. Practically no articles were ever published on the international work of these foreign architects, as if to diminish their stature.

The only exception to this unwritten rule concerned Le Corbusier, who was constantly praised for his artistic qualities and attacked for his alleged political positions. Le Corbusier was the first foreign architect to have obtained an important commission in the USSR—with the exception of Poeltzig, who designed a textile plant in Leningrad in 1927. The evolution of Le Corbusier's Centrosoiuz commission was characteristic of foreign architectural activity in the USSR.

LE CORBUSIER AND THE TSENTROSOIUZ PROJECT

In 1928, Soviet authorities decided to hold a competition to select the architect for the projected headquarters of the Tsentrosoiuz; among the architects invited to take part in the competition was Le Corbusier. On October 30, 1928, Soviet architects who had been invited to enter the competition wrote to the Tsentrosoiuz administration suggesting that the construction of the largest Soviet building ever built should be entrusted to "one of the guiding lights of Western European architecture because we think that the building to be designed will represent, in the clearest possible way, the newest architectural ideas.''[30] Thus Le Corbusier was put in charge of this important commission.

However, the story of the Tsentrosoiuz is also one of how Le Corbusier gradually became dispossessed of this commission. Hailed in the Soviet Union during the 1920s as the leading figure of modern architecture, Le Corbusier progressively became a living symbol of "capitalist" design. When commissioned by Soviet authorities, the Tsentrosoiuz was seen as the expression of the "new communist culture," but while it was under construction, a Soviet planner, S. M. Gornyi, presented it as proof of Le Corbusier's refusal to see Soviet reality. The "proof " of Le Corbusier's "ivory-tower" and "away-from-the-people" attitude was that—as in all air-conditioned buildings—the windows were designed not to be opened![31]

According to another Soviet critic, Le Corbusier did worse than design windows that could not be opened; in his article "Vers une architecture" Le Corbusier wrote the unacceptable phrase "Architecture ou révolution." In 1936, David Arkin, a well-known Soviet architectural critic and formerly a firm supporter of Le Corbusier, wrote about the town-planning ideas of the man he once admired:

[Le Corbusier's] whole proposal concerns not only the rationalization of the city's center. According [to him] this proposal is expected to solve the deepest social contradictions of the contemporary city and to solve them through architecture. This is one of the most cherished, the most often repeated ideas of Le Corbusier. [According to him] the main reason for the dissatisfaction of the masses [living in the towns] is the result of bad housing conditions. This can be solved by peaceful means, by means of architecture. In Le Corbusier's theory, urbanism is not only the adaptation of all aspects of city life to the needs of the Stock Exchange, it is also the way to eradicate all the contradictions of the city that so [worry] the City Bosses. [This is why] he constantly warns the shortsighted and the conservatives: "Architecture or revolution!" The architectural transformation of life can make the social revolution unnecessary. This is how he concludes his book, *On peut éviter la Révolution* [p. 230]. . . . A double task was assigned Le Corbusier by the culture of imperialism: the ultimate liquidation of the preimperialist past and the stabilization [of society] at no matter what cost. This is the social meaning of Le Corbusier's urban theories. Urbanism, which he at first painted in revolutionary colors, . . . has revealed itself to be a set of conservative and defensive ideas.[32]

Le Corbusier never saw the Tsentrosoiuz project completed, other than in photographs supplied by the French embassy in Moscow. In 1929, the All-Union Association of

Proletarian Architects (Vsesoiuznoe Obedinenie Proletar-skikh Arkhitektorov, or VOPRA), which was the equivalent of the unions that already existed for writers, poets, and painters, issued its first manifesto denouncing the construc-tivists for their "mechanical approach"—precisely the func-tionalist approach of European modern architects. Thus when VOPRA criticized unnamed constructivists for their disre-gard of the artistic and ideological aspects of architecture, it was criticizing Western European modern architects, such as May, Le Corbusier, and even Meyer, a communist sym-pathizer.

HANNES MEYER AND THE RISE OF VOPRA

Hannes Meyer's writings reveal a discrepancy between the architectural concepts he developed at the Bauhaus and then tried to promote in the Soviet Union and the prevailing Soviet architectural thought based on socialist realism. Meyer tried to establish rules outlining a materialist and Marxist theory of architecture, which he believed was necessary and possible in a socialist society. In 1928 he wrote:

Building is a biological process. Building is not an aesthetic process. . . . To think of architecture in functional and biological terms . . . leads logically to pure construction: These built-forms have no homeland; they are the expression of an international current of building ideas. One of the qualities of our time is its interna-tionalism.[33]

In a document dated June 13, 1931, that was unpublished at the time, Meyer went farther in denying that any artistic meaning could be derived from the architecture of socialism: "The socialist building is neither beautiful nor ugly; it is either complete or incomplete, worthy or unworthy. The result of an organizational process does not depend on an aesthetic judgment."[34] In defending his opinion that an "artless" nature characterizes socialist architecture, Meyer refuted the domi-nant Soviet architectural thought at the beginning of the 1930s.

In 1930, the constructivist journal *Sovremennaia arkhitektura* was replaced by *Sovetskaia arkhitektura*. In this journal, Ni-kolai A. Miliutin attacked the constructivists whom he had earlier supported in his book, *Sotsgorod*. None of this was understood by the newly arrived architects from Western Europe; they thought that, as in the 1920s, the USSR was still the country where modern architecture was the official architecture. A manifesto was published by VOPRA in August 1929 in the politico-literary journal *Pechat i revoliutsiia* (Writing and revolution):

> We stand for a proletarian art that... expresses the ideas and profound aspirations of the working class.... We stand for a proletarian architecture, for an art that unifies form and content....
> [W]e are for the appropriation of the culture of the past, for the study of its methods through a Marxist analysis... for a critical utilization of historical experience.[35]

Soon the former leaders of VOPRA assumed ruling positions in the Union of Soviet Architects, which was created in 1932. This development followed the dissolution of all *tvorcheskie organizatsii* (creative organizations), including architectural associations, such as constructivist groups, as well as other literary and artistic groups. The new Soviet position rejected constructivism in particular and modern architecture in general. Instead, it embraced what had been considered a backward position among progressive architects: architecture was an art and a way to transmit ideas.

ERNST MAY AND SOVIET PUBLIC HOUSING

A Central Committee resolution published in *Pravda* on May 29, 1930—just after May and his team arrived in Moscow—signified the end of the debate between the urbanists and deurbanists and condemned most of the researchers who had been linked to the idea of *perestroika byta* during the 1920s:

> The Central Committee notes that together with the movement toward a socialist way of life, highly unsound, semifantastical, and hence extremely harmful attempts are being made by certain comrades (Sabsovich, Larin, and others) to surmount "in one leap" the obstacles that lie along the path to a socialist transformation of the way of life; obstacles rooted, on the one hand, in the economic and cultural backwardness of the country and, on the other, in the need, at our present stage of development, to concentrate most of our resources on the rapid industrialization that alone will create the necessary material basis for a radical transformation of the way of life. These attempts on the part of certain militants, who conceal their opportunism behind the "left-wing phrase," are linked with recently published projects for the reorganization of existing cities and the construction of new ones. The implementation of these harmful and utopian proposals, which disregard both the actual resources of the country and the degree of preparation of the population, would lead to vast expenditures of money and would se-

riously discredit the very idea of a socialist transformation of the way of life.[36]

May probably did not realize the significance of this resolution.

Unlike Le Corbusier, May and his brigade worked on housing projects and the public buildings directly related to such projects—the type of projects that had made May famous in Frankfurt. May did not try to introduce "revolutionary" architectural forms; he understood that he had to adapt himself to the low level of the Soviet Union's building technology and labor force. This was easy for him because his style of architecture was extremely simple in terms of form. On the other hand, May relied on rather advanced technology, which he thought he could adapt to Soviet conditions in order to speed up housing construction in the USSR. The need for housing construction was tremendous all over the Soviet Union, particularly in new industrial settlements, such as Magnitogorsk. In this "new town," one hundred thousand inhabitants, most of whom lived in temporary shelters, were already at work in 1930 when May was put in charge of town planning. In the planning of Magnitogorsk, May applied the principles that he had used in Frankfurt and that architects of the modern movement had used throughout Western Europe: parallel rows of identical buildings were built at equal distances, thus giving each inhabitant optimal conditions for sunshine and light.

For May, as for Gropius and other modern architects, uniformity was the symbolic—as well as the material—sign of the egalitarian living conditions that were to exist in housing, particularly socialist housing. In the Soviet Union, this form of planning had other advantages: it simplified the work of topographical crews; it made the use of mechanical equipment—particularly cranes—easier; and, like a factory assembly line, it made the most efficient use of untrained Soviet manpower. The result was a rather monotonous form of architecture and town planning. This was less apparent in Germany, where the development of surrounding areas compensated for uniform architecture and town planning; in the Soviet Union, a general shortage of materials and manpower and a rapid pace of construction precluded the development of such compensating areas.

Thus the quality of housing, as well as the quality of roads, sewers, and other constructions designed by foreign architectural teams in the USSR, could not be compared with the results obtained by the same team in Germany. Junghanns cites a striking example of this situation: "The masonry of the kindergartens in Magnitogorsk was executed by Kirghiz girls who had arrived directly from the tents of the nomads. The brigadier spoke only Kirghiz and could not read the blueprints. . . . Mart Stam [a Dutch architect belonging to May's team], who was accustomed to the very precise work of Dutch bricklayers and who had accepted being sent to Magnitogorsk to supervise the execution of the project, gave up after a short time."[37] May's job was made more difficult because Soviet authorities were constantly changing their plans. For example, in the case of Magnitogorsk, S. Ordzhonikidze decided on which bank of the Ural River to build the city long after May's team had begun working on the town plan.[38]

ANDRÉ LURCAT AND HANNES MEYER:
POLITICS AND ARCHITECTURE

Among foreign architects working in the USSR, Lurcat represents a unique case because his first contacts with the USSR were political rather than architectural in nature. In addition, Lurcat settled in the USSR in 1934, long after most of the prominent German architects had left the Soviet Union and after Le Corbusier's de facto break in relations with Soviet specialists. In 1934, there could have been no illusions about the fact that the orientation of Soviet architecture differed radically from the expectations of the modernists. The Union of Soviet Architects, which had proclaimed socialist realism as the theory for all Soviet architects, was firmly installed. Heading it were former VOPRA leaders, including A. Mordvinov and K. Alabian.

When Lurcat left for the USSR—a country he had already visited as a "friend of the Soviet Union"—he knew that his style of architecture, exemplified by the school in Villejuif, had been criticized and presented as the architectural expression of "capitalist decay." In fact, Lurcat's work in the USSR reveals a steady evolution toward an acceptance of the new trend in Soviet architecture and a rejection of the principles he had defended before going to the USSR. The explanation of this architectural reversal may be related to his political convictions, because as a Communist he was compelled to support the Soviet regime in his writings and his work.

Hannes Meyer, on the other hand, continued to support

the USSR in his writings after leaving the Soviet Union in 1936, but not the slightest trace of the architectural principles he had defended during his last years in the USSR can be found in his later work. In 1933, in *Arkhitektura SSSR* (Architecture of the USSR), he expressed an apparent acceptance of the new order: "Recently I have again been interested in classical and, more generally, ancient architecture while exploring for myself the problem of 'national expression' in socialist architecture."[39] Although Meyer initially tried to demonstrate that architecture was not an art, his views evolved toward the new Soviet position on architecture. In 1934, he was interviewed by *Sovetskaia arkhitektura*:

Sovetskaia arkhitektura: How do you feel about the rejection of art in housing and town planning by those architects who call themselves progressive thinkers?
Meyer: I consider the rejection of art in the field of construction by some contemporary capitalist architects as one of the signs of the crumbling of "bourgeois" culture.

In the same interview, Meyer counterposed the "progressive" period of "bourgeois" society with its present period of decay. Commenting on his previous opinions, he added:

We, the architects, did then consider the social aspect as the main aspect of architecture, and we called this architecture "functional." It is therefore not surprising that these efforts to reform "bourgeois" architecture ended up with, at best, purely mechanical results.

To defend a progressive point of view in architecture means to share a political program that is developed on the barricades and not on the drawing board.[40]

But Meyer's return to the architectural principles he established during his time at the Bauhaus can be seen in his later projects in Mexico, where he worked as an architect, town planner, and professor at the newly created Town Planning Institute.

Lurcat, however, applied aspects of socialist realism in his work in France following the Second World War.[41] Apparently, he sincerely believed in the theory of socialist realism, and he believed that it represented progress over the radical modernist positions he had supported during the 1920s. In his great housing projects for Saint-Denis and other communist municipalities of the Paris region, as well as for the town of Maubeuge where he was in charge of the postwar reconstruction, Lurcat introduced *la grande composition*—a concept adapted from the Ecole des beaux arts and later discussed by specialists in Moscow. This was in total contradiction to his early 1930s work on the Groupe scolaire Karl Marx in Villejuif.

The discrepancy between the theory of socialist realism and the personal architectural beliefs of the majority of foreign architects in the Soviet Union is apparent in the attitude the foreign community displayed toward the "new trend" in Soviet architecture, which became dominant after 1930. This discrepancy became evident to most of the modern architectural community during the 1932 competition for the Palace of Soviets in Moscow, and the break between foreign and Soviet architects occurred at that time and lasted until 1956.

THE PALACE OF SOVIETS COMPETITION AND ITS AFTERMATH

The international competition for the Palace of Soviets building was launched in 1931, and all the major modern architects were invited to participate. Before the results were announced, the majority of architects believed Le Corbusier's entry would be the winning project. But to everyone's amazement, the proclaimed winner was Boris Iofan, a relatively unknown Soviet architect. From his studies in Italy, Iofan had retained some knowledge of the architectural principles of the Renaissance, and his project contradicted the fundamental principles of modern architecture.

Coincidentally, at precisely the time the announcement was made, a CIAM commission was meeting in Barcelona to prepare for its fourth congress, which was to be held in Moscow on the theme of the functional city. One member of this preparatory commission was V. M. Molotov. Astonished by the result of the competition, the CIAM commission believed—or pretended to believe—that it was a mistake, an error of judgment by some irresponsible minor commission. In a letter addressed to Stalin, the CIAM commission asked the Soviet authorities to rectify the error:

The verdict of the committee for the construction of the Soviet Palace is a direct insult to the spirit of the Russian Revolution and to the Five-Year Plan. Turning its back on the ideas of modern society, which has found its first inspiration in Soviet Russia, this verdict offers support to the pretentious architecture of the former monarchist regime. The Soviet Palace, proposed to the modern world as the spiritual crowning of the immense and rational achievements of the Five-Year Plan, will demonstrate the enslavement of modern techniques for the greatest benefit of spiritual reaction. The

Soviet Palace . . . will appear to totally disregard the gigantic efforts of modern times. A dramatic betrayal! The world that is watching the Soviet experiment will be astounded. . . . The CIRPAC [the preparatory commission] asks the supreme Soviet authority to intervene, for, if the decision of the committee were to be followed, it would become doubtful that the CIRPAC, engaged to advance public opinion by its previous positions and its objectives, could continue to consider that the USSR was the country most fit to shelter a fruitful congress on a subject that can bear no compromise: "The Functional City."[42]

But the Soviet "supreme" authority did not intervene, for it was precisely this supreme authority that had decided to make the Palace of Soviets competition a manifesto for the new direction Soviet architecture was to take. Nor did Stalin answer this letter. The fourth CIAM finally took place, not in Moscow, but on a cruise ship in Athens in the summer of 1934. The Athens Charter, which resulted from the congress, remains a controversial theoretical document on modern town planning.

The CIAM's direct intervention into what some considered an internal Soviet affair met with the disapproval of a group of German architects still at work in the USSR. Many of them believed that the Soviet reversal *(povorot)* was only a temporary concession to the poor tastes of uncultured masses. Nevertheless, in increasing numbers, these specialists decided that the time had come to leave the USSR. The incompatibility between even their simplest plans and prevailing Soviet conditions was too great. Moreover, beginning with the second Five-Year Plan in 1933, the Soviet authorities apparently decided that the foreigners' experience in the USSR must come to an end and that foreign architecture was neither desirable nor possible under existing Soviet conditions. Suspicion of foreign architects grew during the second half of the 1930s, and by 1937, the overwhelming majority of foreign architects had left the Soviet Union.

As if to put an end to the period when foreign architects were considered useful to the industrialization of the Soviet Union, A. Mostakov, a former Soviet member of May's team, wrote an article entitled, "The Ugly Heritage of the Architect E. May":

When receiving delegates to the First Congress of Soviet Architects [1937], V. Molotov is reported to have said that architects do not often criticize the defects in their colleagues' projects, as in the case of "the ugly heritage of the architect E. May." . . . One hardly can congratulate the directors of the Tsekombank who invited the architect E. May for this responsible task [housing the masses]. They neither studied nor critically appraised [his work in Frankfurt]. None of them considered that, contrary to the capitalist city, the conception of a housing ensemble in our country cannot be separated from the conception of the city as a whole. Soviet architects made an unforgivable mistake by giving Ernst May the opportunity to design and to build on a vast scale without critically observing his work. E. May was commissioned to design not only housing but also whole sectors, towns, and even regions, although he knew perfectly well that the totality of his creative "baggage" *[bagazh]* was nothing but a few blocks in Frankfurt. As one knows, May has designed all his projects by applying the method of "linear composition." What is this method "patented" by the German functionalists: Hesler, Gropius, Taut and May himself?

Furthermore, Mostakov explains the drawbacks of linear composition, or *strochnaia zastroika:*

The result of this method is the equality of living conditions [which one would think should please a socialist architect]. This is real "housing socialism" [Mostakov says ironically]. One must say that many architects were satisfied with this vulgar and purely mechanical approach!... But what is the most vulgar mistake made by May and his followers? What is the organic evil of his conception? It lies, above all, in the fact that May excludes man *[chelovek]* from his architectural conception. He replaces the human personality with some sort of a sum of biological and technological requirements... and responds to these requirements with purely mechanical solutions that reduce the complex notion of housing *[zhilishche]* to the primitive concept of "function." There lies the reason for his "boxlike" primitivism that May passes off as "contemporary housing." May is pursuing one goal: to present the human creature as a soulless and abstract "number" by ignoring the cultural development of Soviet citizens and by imposing upon them a "petit bourgeois" *[melkoburzhuaznuiu]* psychology. May was hiding his creative incapacity and the narrow limits of his thoughts behind demagogical sentences about standardized projects, economy, and hygiene. Does not his [Moscow reconstruction] proposal involving satellite communities connected by a linear system of transportation and isolated from the town center pursue the objective of dispersing the workers of the capital?[43]

May did not have experience in town planning, but few in those days did. And May provided the workers who were to inhabit the new Soviet industrial settlements with the only living conditions possible given the Soviet economy at that time. Mostakov accused him of not creating an ideal city, even though the achievement of that ideal was totally beyond the scope of Soviet capabilities during the 1930s. Moreover, Mostakov condemned May for having done this on purpose, for political reasons. But while Mostakov was writing the above article, May left the Soviet Union.

The extent to which the projects of foreign architects in the USSR have been built in conformity with their original designs is unknown; evidently no study exists on this subject, and the rare available photographs and plans of the new industrial cities of the first two Five-Year Plans bear little resemblance to the finished projects. Reproductions of these projects are also scarce. For this reason, it is difficult to reach conclusions regarding the quality and usefulness of work done by foreign architects in the USSR and the practical effects of their work on the development of Soviet architecture. Of the projects designed by May, Meyer, and other German and German-speaking architects, few were actually constructed. A few buildings designed by Lurcat are scattered throughout the Moscow area. Regardless of how important the Tsentrosoiuz commission might have been in its time, it represents an isolated case of visible foreign involvement in Soviet architecture.

ALBERT KAHN: ONE AMERICAN'S FRUITFUL COOPERATION WITH THE SOVIET UNION

Considering the political climate existing between the Soviet Union and the United States during the 1930s—a period marked by the absence of diplomatic relations, the growth of "left-wing" movements in the United States because of the Depression, and the "red scare" hysteria remaining from the end of the First World War—it is surprising that architectural cooperation between the United States and the USSR achieved the most spectacular results.

The main actor was Albert Kahn. Kahn's firm designed most of the automobile plants in Michigan, particularly those of Henry Ford, to whom Kahn was personally connected. From the time he signed a contract with the Soviets in April 1929 until he ended his cooperation with Soviet authorities in March 1932, Kahn's firm designed about 520 industrial plants in the Soviet Union.[44] Many of these were built in almost inaccessible and uninhabited areas—an environment that contrasted sharply with conditions under which American architectural technicians were accustomed to working. Kahn was among the few foreign architects in the Soviet Union to become widely known by the Soviet population. During the Second World War, Philip A. Adler of the *Detroit News* wrote from Stalingrad: "The names of Henry Ford and

Albert Kahn are known to every child in Stalingrad. John K. Calder who supervised the reconversion of the city, at one time was the hero of Soviet stage and screen."[45]

There was no trace of a common ideological or political belief between Kahn and the Communist Party or Soviet government. In this respect, Kahn differed from the German architects of the *neues Bauen,* Lurcat, and even Le Corbusier. Kahn displayed no curiosity concerning "the greatest national experiment" or interest in the "birthplace" of modern architecture. Kahn's architectural writings show that he had a great dislike for modern architecture, which he called "ultra modern," and especially for Soviet modern architecture. This dislike is surprising because Kahn, the greatest industrial architect of his day, designed factories on a rigorous assembly-line system—very close to what Gropius had imagined for the Fagus Factory in Germany[46] and in line with the principles advocated by the functionalists and Russian constructivists. Nevertheless, Kahn was a strong supporter of traditional architecture; he did not believe that "our times" called for new forms of architectural expression. According to Kahn, "the styles" were only a vast catalogue from which architects and clients could choose at random. In 1931, he said:

I have little patience with those who claim [Charles F. McKim's] work [is] archeology and not architecture. Indeed he found his inspiration in the past, but he knew how to employ the best of the old to do service to the new. . . . I insist that the reuse of well tried forms when invigorated by a strong personality is not unobjectionable but desirable, the opinion of many of our modernists to the contrary notwithstanding.[47]

According to Kahn, modern architecture would have remained unknown and unnoticed if not for the media:

Probably no one has done more injury than Le Corbusier and his followers. Only those who have actually seen the finished results can appreciate the difference between their theories and their accomplishments. But for the writers who too often laud their abortive attempts to the skies, form wrong public opinion and cause an era of misunderstanding, their sad creations would probably receive but little notice. . . . There seems little reason for acclaiming the "Dessau Bauhaus," for instance, as outstanding. Is it architecture at all? We may find in this country hundreds of factory buildings, particularly the court or alley elevations where often there has been no attempt whatever at design, just as uninteresting, just as devoid of architectural feeling. Though credited with assisting in some measure the new vogue in the treatment of the modern factory building by clearly expressing what it is and capitalizing on its purely inherent possibilities, I would be the last man to claim the results as anything more than sound engineering unless the problem and the appropriation afforded a more architectural character.[48]

Ironically, this was written just as an exhibition of modern architecture, which was to have a decisive influence on the evolution of American architecture, opened at the Museum of Modern Art in New York.[49]

Thus for purely technical reasons—and not because of his architectural theories or political opinions—Kahn became the most influential and productive foreign architect in the Soviet Union. In the spring of 1929, a top-level Soviet economic and technical commission traveled to Detroit to study the American automobile industry and discovered that most of the plants had been designed by Louis Kahn, Albert Kahn's brother. This visit led to the signing of a $40 million contract for the construction of a tractor plant in Stalingrad with the Amtorg Trading Corporation—a Russian commercial trading organization. The importance accorded to the tractor and automobile industry in the USSR was clearly linked to the political importance attached to agriculture and town planning at the end of the 1920s and beginning of the 1930s. In 1929, collectivization, which was predicated on the mechanization of agriculture, was in full swing, and this required the large-scale production of tractors. In the field of urban planning, the discussions between the urbanists and deurbanists seemed to have turned in favor of the deurbanists, whose schemes leaned heavily on automobile transportation.

The Stalingrad tractor commission was soon followed by many others,[50] and an American technical team from the Detroit office was soon installed in Moscow and headed by Kahn's brother, Moritz. This team of about thirty American technicians was to be in charge of designing new projects, while at the same time acting as a sort of professional school for Soviet technicians. The team instructed about fifteen hundred Soviets, only some of whom had professional qualifications.

Although he lacked political affinity for the Soviet Union, Kahn felt sympathy for the country and its people: "Everywhere throughout Russia I found the people, particularly the young, not only satisfied with the Soviet form of government, but firmly convinced the officials at its head are sincere and honest."[51] "In my trip through Russia . . . I was struck by the tremendous enthusiasm and energy of the people, especially the young, everywhere in this nationwide development."[52] Recalling a meeting with Kahn after Kahn's return from Russia in 1932, Malcom W. Bingay wrote in the *Detroit Free Press* in 1942:

This quiet, modest gentleman had been commissioned by the Soviet government in 1929 to plan their great factories, the products of which—behind the Ural Mountains—are now holding the Nazis at bay. I remember what he said when he came back from Moscow in 1932, just ten years ago. He said then: "There is little communism in Russia today and no one can tell what Sovietism will stand for ten years from now."[53]

In the same article, Bingay talks about Kahn's relations with Henry Ford and Ford's attitude in the 1930s toward the Soviet Union:

Now, it was a daring thing for Albert Kahn to accept that commission to Russia in the face of American public opinion, for very few Americans wanted their names associated with those "awful people." But he immediately got moral support from a wholly unexpected source.

The day it was announced that he had signed his contract his largest customer in the designing of factories, Henry Ford, called him on the phone and asked him to see him before he sailed.

"Mr. Ford," said Mr. Kahn, "was just leaving with his wife for a trip to the Virginia colonial settlement at Williamsburg. 'I hear,' he said, 'that you have agreed to build factories for the Russian Government. I am very glad of it. I have been thinking that these people should be helped.'

"I could hardly believe my ears, but Mr. Ford continued: 'I think the stabilization of Russia through industry is the hope of the world. The more industry we can create, the more men and women, the world over, can be made self sufficient—the more everybody will benefit. The Russian people have a right to their destiny and they can only find it through work. We are willing out here to help them all we can.

" 'So you tell them for me that anything we have is theirs for the asking—free. They can have our designs, our work methods, our steel specifications—anything. We will send them our engineers to teach them and they can send their men into our plants to learn.' "[54]

Kahn recalled that he had hesitated before accepting the commission in Russia:

I was somewhat hesitant about accepting such a task. First, I knew little or nothing about the Russian government and the people behind it. Second, the United States had refused to recognize that government. Third, there was a feeling against Communists among the people with whom I had to do business. Fourth, the enemies of my people echoed what the Nazis were saying and accused the Jews of fostering Communism. I wondered what would be said if I took the job. And yet the challenge fascinated me. . . . I believed that the Russian people—regardless of their form of government—were entitled to help after all their generations of suffering under the czars. The more I thought about it the more I became convinced it was the right thing to do.[55]

In January 1944, Louis Kahn, who had become president of the firm after his brother's death in 1942, reflected on how he and his brother had regarded the possibility of working with the Russians in 1929:

Representatives of the Soviet government approached us early in 1929 with a proposal that we help them industrialize the vast potential manufacturing resources. We felt at that time as we feel today, that the industrialization of other countries would help the world generally, just as it has raised the living standard in America. In this attitude we were encouraged by many enlightened business leaders whose cooperation in training Russians in the techniques of mass production was essential to the success of the overall enterprise. . . .
[The Russians] exhibited a faith in the honesty and ability of Americans which should put us on guard to make sure, in all our dealing with them, that our own skirts are completely clean. Seldom has the Albert Kahn organization had a more pleasant or finer contractual relationship than with the Soviet government. If any question of business dealings with Russia arises, and if any doubter comes to us, he will be told, out of our personal experience, that "We have done business with Russia, and we can do business with Russia."[56]

The Kahns had a financial interest in working in the Soviet Union because at that time commissions in the United States had become scarce. In America during the Depression, factory construction practically came to a standstill. This led thousands of Americans to think about going to work in the USSR, where technicians and qualified workers were being recruited, despite the fact that there were no diplomatic relations between the Soviet Union and the United States. Thousands of letters—today stored in the National Archives in Washington, D.C.—poured into the Department of State. Some were naive. One pleaded, "I would be very grateful if you could direct me to someone who could get me in touch with some firm that is hiring young college graduates for work in Russia on this new Five-Year Plan that the country is fostering at present."[57] Another said:

I would appreciate it very much if you would let me know what the living conditions are in that country and whether or not a young man of nineteen years of age, an American, could be happy there. I also understand that our country does not recognize the Soviet Government and that we have no representation there. If you will let me have the real facts as to conditions in Russia, I would appreciate it very much, as I do not want my son, who is making application, to leave the United States.[58]

Some, like the following telegram, were matter-of-fact: "I am an experienced Railroad man and I am interested in Railroad work in Russia."[59] Some were tragic, reflecting the situation of unemployed Americans during the Great Depression (original spelling has been maintained):

I have read in the *Cincinati Post* that Amerika is sending men with treades over in Russia for a term of 3 Jeahrs with a pay of 3500 $ per Jeahr and, as business is Poor I would like to find out where I would have to apply for a Position as construction foremann or Carpenter for a term as mentioned before. I hope to hear from you soon as I am idle and dont like to be so. I speak English and German.[60]

In the following letter addressed to the Department of State, reason can be found for Kahn's hesitation in accepting the Soviet commission:

In the Saturday Evening Post, March 7th, page 24, appears an editorial headed "The American Five-Year Plan." May I ask the State Department if it has a list of these Americans who are giving aid, comfort, credit & etc. to the Soviet Government, and if so may I ask that a copy be sent me? Is there no law, or rule that could be invoked to deny reentry to the United States to these men, their agents, et al?[61]

In 1932, Soviet-American architectural cooperation ended. Because of a shortage of foreign currency in the USSR, a new policy was implemented that governed commercial relations with foreign firms. Beginning in 1932, payments were to be made partly in rubles; prior to 1932 payments had been made entirely in foreign currency. According to the *Detroit Free Press:*

Recent cables from Russia report a veritable exodus of American specialists as a result of a new policy under which many individual technical aid contracts, specifying large payments in dollars, are being terminated on one ground or another. Some contracts are not being renewed. In other cases, the Soviet is trying to get some specialists to agree to remain for normal payments in dollars or large payments in rubles, which are not usable outside the Soviet Union.

"It is only natural that they should try to drive sharp bargains," said Mr. Kahn. "They, like us, are upset by the Depression. My firm, of course, would prefer to be paid in dollars. . . . Besides, the Soviet has met with a great many trade obstacles in the United States, and I believe that today Germany is a preferred nation. We do not anticipate, however, any alteration in our pleasant business relations."[62]

On March 25, 1932, the *New York Times* reported on Kahn's departure from the USSR:

Albert Kahn left Moscow tonight, unable to renew his contract to teach the Russians technical and architectural designing, which legally terminated March 1 but had been held open in the hope that a renewal might be effected upon mutually satisfactory terms. 24 Americans employed in the Kahn office here will follow their chief within the next fortnight. Mr. Kahn told the writer he deeply regretted his failure to reach an agreement.

"They want us to stay and feel we have done valuable work," he said. "They proposed to employ 40 of our people here instead of 24 and to open branch offices at Kharkov and Leningrad, but we simply couldn't meet them on terms.

"We part company in the friendliest spirit, however, and I hope and believe the connection will be resumed when the circumstances permit."[63]

This marked the end of what had been by far the most fruitful cooperation between Soviet authorities and foreign architects and technicians. Kahn's success—in contrast to the general inability of other foreign architects to exert influence on the course of Soviet architecture—can be explained in part by the fact that Kahn's organization was able to work on its Soviet projects on both sides of the Atlantic. If something was missing in Russia, Kahn had it sent from America,[64] whereas May, for example, was relatively cut off from his home country in terms of receiving both technical information and material supplies. In addition, Kahn's factory assignments were simpler than May's town-planning projects. Moreover, a housing development or town might be inhabited before May had finished his work, thereby obstructing construction; but a factory—especially one built using the assembly-line system—had to be completed according to strict schedules imposed by the Five-Year Plan. Finally, Kahn's work was not hampered by ideological discussions, probably because of the great need for building factories during the late 1920s and early 1930s. During this period, there was an abundance of literature on workers' clubs, housing projects, town and regional planning, and architectural theories and history, but the literature concerning industrial plants remained purely technical in nature. Although almost all areas of Soviet culture became ideological battlefields during the 1930s and the analytical methods used in politics were directly applied to the arts, architecture, human sciences, and even to some scientific fields, industrial architecture remained undiscussed and unattacked from an ideological point of view.

Neither during Kahn's period of activity in the Soviet Union nor since his departure—when Western art, ideology, and life-styles came under fire—has his work been the object of any sort of criticism. Moreover, of all the foreign architects who worked in the Soviet Union, Albert Kahn was apparently the only one to whom homage was rendered after his death. The following telegram from the Soviet embassy in Washington was sent to Albert Kahn's widow when he died on December 8, 1942:

Soviet engineers, builders, and architects send you their sincere sympathy in connection with the death of your husband, Mr. Albert Kahn, who rendered us great service in designing a number of large plants and helped us to assimilate the American experience in the sphere of building industry. Soviet engineers and architects will always warmly remember the name of the talented American engineer and architect, Albert Kahn.[65]

The telegram was signed by V. A. Vesnin, architect, academician. Victor Vesnin was one of the three Vesnin brothers, a well-known family team of modern, constructivist architects.

OTHER AMERICAN ARCHITECTS IN THE SOVIET UNION

Isadore Rosenfield, a well-known American architect specializing in hospital construction, worked in the Soviet Union during the 1930s, although little is known regarding his activity there. He wrote an article for *Soviet Russia Today* on his impressions of Soviet architecture in 1935:[66]

In 1932 I traveled exclusively in the Soviet Union studying housing and socialist city planning. Speaking Russian and traveling third category, often unaccompanied, there was little that escaped my attention. (No one tried to keep anything from me.) During the winter of 1933–34 I collaborated in the planning of the All-Union Institute of Experimental Medicine. In May 1934, I returned to Moscow to assist with the survey preliminary to construction of the U. S. Embassy there. For the past several months I have been representing in this country the architectural-technical commission for the Palace of the Soviets.

According to Rosenfield, the purpose of architecture in capitalist countries was "to glorify the rich or advertise their wares," whereas

in the Soviet Union the purpose of architecture is altogether different. There its purpose is to provide shelter for living, production and cultural activity for and by the broad masses of the workers. Instead of advertising individual greed, it proclaims the glory of its great leaders and symbolizes the solidarity of united labor. The architects and builders there are not exploiters, but participants in the united program of socialist construction.

This was a transitional period in Soviet architecture, and Rosenfield defended the new trend. He criticized modernist architecture, which he claimed "in a sense represents an 'intellectual revolt' against dogmatism," but "the ideologies which were wound around this architecture [are] mere flowers around a corpse." According to Rosenfield, modernism was acceptable during the first years of industrialization:

The people in the Soviet Union during the first Five-Year Plan also faced the problem of building quickly with limited materials, limited skill and limited experience. The boxy style of modernism was the logical answer to these conditions. [This] boxy style . . . was further induced by the influence of many pseudo-radical architects who flocked to Russia in order to escape the Depression. "Pseudo-radicals" because most of them believed they could usher in the millennium by introducing modernism in all phases of technology. . . . Cheap and nasty architecture . . . did not suit the workers of the Soviets. Nor did it suit them in art, literature, sculpture, etc. Accordingly, the communist party and the government of the Soviet Union passed a resolution on the eve of the Second Five-Year Plan in which they called [for] an end to boxes and the inauguration of more culture in all forms of art as well as in architecture.

Rosenfield believes that the new trend in Soviet architecture—the rejection of modern architecture in favor of a renewed interest in classical architecture—was justified. Finally, he concludes the article in a "populist" manner:

In a recent number of *Arkhitectura,* the official organ of the Union of Soviet architects, dozens of letters from workers are printed. They made marvelous reading for they tell the architects in a simple, direct manner what they like and what they don't like, and why. They do not even care if they hurt some architect's feelings. Why should they? It is their country.

A few other American architects were employed by Soviet organizations. In 1935, Abraham Luline of New York City was employed by the Steelbridge Construction Trust of Sverdlovsk; Louis Harry Friedheim of Brooklyn, New York, was employed by the Sverdlovsk city soviet; and Abraham Schwartz, also of Brooklyn, was employed by the Moscow Industrial Construction Desofu Bureau. In 1936, William U. Rixford of Wellsville, New York, was employed by the Moscow Industrial Construction Trust, and in 1937, Joseph Winston of New York City worked in the Soviet Union, although his employer remains unknown. In addition, a number of construction workers, carpenters, and bricklayers appear on the lists of American citizens residing in the USSR that were compiled by the American embassy in Moscow from 1935–39,[67] but there is nothing in these lists regarding the activity of architects.

WHAT IS TO BE DONE?

Today the belief that architecture could be a tool of social transformation might seem naive. But this belief, widely shared by architectural avant-gardists during the interwar period, provides a major clue to understanding the "progressive" architecture of the 1920s and 1930s. Many of the utopian experiments that gave rise to this belief took place in the United States during the nineteenth century, and were inspired by utopian thinkers such as Fourier, Owen, Cabet, and Bellamy.[68]

But during the first decades of the twentieth century, many thought that the country where these experiments would reach a definitive and positive conclusion was the Soviet Union. To the foreign architects working in the Soviet Union during the 1920s and 1930s, utopia seemed a necessary part of architecture. As early as 1862–63, Nikolai Chernyshevskii described the city of the future in *What Is to Be Done?*. Responding to the question, "And will all people live that way?" he answered:

Yes . . . for all an everlasting spring and summer, an everlasting joy! You know the future. It is bright, it is beautiful. Tell everybody. Here is what is to be! The future is bright and beautiful. Love it! Seek to reach it! Work for it! Bring it nearer to men! . . . Your life will be bright, beautiful, rich with happiness and enjoyment. . . . Strive to reach it! Work for it! Bring it nearer to men. Transfer from it into the present all that you are able to transfer![69]

In December 1954 First Secretary Nikita Khrushchev criticized the "new trend" in Soviet architecture, and in the summer of 1956 relations between the Soviet and foreign architectural communities were reestablished, after having been interrupted as a consequence of the Palace of Soviets verdict. The resumption of relations was a result of a visit to the USSR by a delegation of French architects.[70] Since the 1960s, the brilliant and inventive architecture of the 1920s has been progressively "rehabilitated" by Soviet and foreign architectural historians.

NOTES

1. Kurt Junghanns, "Deutsche Architekten in der Sowjet Union während der erste Fünfjahrplan und des Vaterländischen Krieges," in *Wissenschaftliche Zeitschrift der Hochschule für Architektur and Bauwesen* (Weimar) 29, no. 2 (1983).
2. On the Bauhaus heritage in Israel, see Michael Levin, "'White City' International Style Architecture in Israel: A Portrait of an Era" (Catalog to the exhibition in the Tel Aviv Museum, 1984). According to Levin, nineteen former Bauhaus students, seven of whom were architects, settled in Israel after 1933.
3. Foreign publications did not always note which architectural designs were only planned and which were actually built. Hundreds of Soviet architectural projects never left the drafting board.
4. CIAM, an international organization of modern architects that was created in 1928, regularly organized international congresses on the subject of modern architecture and town planning.
5. Excerpted from the manifesto adopted by the first CIAM, held in La Sarraz in 1928.
6. Walter Gropius, *Zentralblatt der Bauverwaltung*, 21 March 1930, no. 12.
7. Le Corbusier, *Précisions sur un etat présent de l'architecture et de l'urbanisme* (Paris: Editions Crès, 1930), 88.
8. Le Corbusier, *La Ville radieuse* (Paris: Editions Vincent, Freal, 1964), 148.
9. Ernst May, "Stadtrat Mays Russland Pläne," *Bauwelt*, 1930, no. 21:1156. Quoted by Kurt Junghanns in "Deutsche Architekten in der Sowjet Union."
10. Ernst May, "Bekenntnisse des Stadtbauers," in *Das neue Russland*, 1930, no. 5–6:53.
11. Walter Gropius, "Was erhoffen wir uns vom russischen Stadtbau," *Das neue Russland*, 1931, no. 6–7:57.
12. As quoted by Kurt Junghanns in "Deutsche Architekten in der Sowjet Union."
13. Neither Le Corbusier nor Lurcat designed any projects other than private villas during the first years of professional practice. In contrast, during the same period, modern German architects were already in charge of important housing and social projects.
14. Ernst May, "Das soziale Moment in der neue Baukunst," *Das neue Frankfurt*, 1928, no. 5.
15. Ernst May, "Das Soziale Moment."
16. Many in Germany believed that architecture already served as a means of shaping society; "counter societies" were created that included

schools, clubs, cultural associations, health centers, and public facilities that might house unemployment insurance agencies, for example. A German anecdote of that period commented, "You can be born in a social democratic maternity and be buried by a social democratic undertaker without ever having left the social democratic world" (quoted from Joseph Rovan, *Histoire de la social-démocratie allemande* [Paris: Seuil, 1978]).

17. Bruno Taut, *Die neue Baukunst in Europa und in Amerika* (Stuttgart, 1929), 54.

18. Quoted from Jean-Pierre Giordani, "Analyse des Documents du Congrès d' Athenes" (Mémoire de Maîtrise à l'Université de Paris VIII, 1980).

19. Moisei Ginzburg, *Sovremennaia arkhitektura,* 1928, no. 5.

20. M. Okhitovitch, "O problemakh goroda," *Sovremennaia arkhitektura,* 1929, no. 4.

21. In rejecting Le Corbusier's project, the international competition in Geneva for the League of Nations building demonstrated that "traditional" architects were still powerful and received political support.

22. Belonging to the original team, which departed on May 8, 1930, were: Hans Burkhart, Mr. Fritsche, Max Fruhof, Gustav Hassenpflug, Wilhelm Hauss, Werner Hedebrand, Mr. Keil, S. Kolpenetzky, Walter Kratz, Karl Lehmann, Hans Leistikow, Albert Locher, Erich Mauthner, Mr. Niemeyer, Hans Schmidt, Walter Schütte, Grete Schütte-Lihotzky, Walter Schulz, Walter Schwagenscheidt, Mart Stam, and Albert Winter. In 1931, Eugen Kaufmann and Kurt Liebknecht joined the team in Moscow. See Walter Schwagenscheidt, *Baukunst und Werkform,* 1956, no. 9:477.

23. El Lissitzky suffered from tuberculosis and was sent to Switzerland for treatment several times during the 1920s. Some of his visits to the Dessau Bauhaus were made during trips to a sanatorium.

24. The Bauhaus delegation was headed by Arieh Sharon, a Bauhaus student from Palestine. Sharon had emigrated from Poland to what was then Palestine under the British mandate and had been sent to study at the Bauhaus by his kibbutz. He later became one of the best-known architects in Israel.

25. *Pravda,* 10 October 1930.

26. Some of the names of May's Soviet coworkers are recorded in Justus Buekschmidt, *Ernst May* (Stuttgart, 1963).

27. *Sovetskaia arkhitektura,* the unofficial organ of VOPRA (All-Union Association of Proletarian Architects), maintained a "political and ideological" orientation, that sought to combat the "leftist" and "rightist" deviations of the constructivists and formalists.

28. Conversation between Grete Schütte-Lihotzky and the author at the Bauhaus Colloquium held at the Hochschule für Architektur und Bauwesen in Weimar, June 1986.

29. *Stroitel'naia promyshlennost',* 1926, no. 6/7.

30. Archives at the Fondation Le Corbusier in Paris, October 29, 1928.

31. Le Corbusier, *Planirovka goroda* (Translation of *Precisions,* with an introduction by S. M. Gornyi) (Moscow, 1933). This accusation was often repeated until modern architecture was "rehabilitated" in the Soviet Union in the early 1960s.

32. David Arkin, "K kharakteristike arkhitekturnykh techenii XX veka na zapade," *Akademia arkhitektury,* 1936, no. 3.

33. Hannes Meyer, *Das Bauhaus* (Dessau, 1928).

34. Hannes Meyer, "Thesen über Marxistische Architektur," in Hannes Meyer, ed., *Bauen und Gesellschaft: Schrifte, Briefe, Projekte* (Dresden: VEB Verlag der Kunst, 1980.).

35. *Pechat' i revoliutsiia*, 1929, no. 6.

36. *Pravda*, 29 May 1930.

37. Junghanns, "Deutsche Architekten in der Sowjet Union."

38. Ernst May, "Stadtbau und Wohnungswesen in der UdSSR nach 30 Jahren," *Bauwelt*, 1960, no. 3:63.

39. Hannes Meyer, "Kak ia rabotaiu," *Arkhitektura SSSR*, 1933, no. 6:35.

40. Hannes Meyer, "Arkhitektor v klassovoi borbe," *Sovetskaia arkhitektura*, 1934, no. 1.

41. On André Lurcat, see Jean-Louis Cohen (Ph. D. diss., l'Ecole des hautes etudes en sciences sociales, 1985).

42. Fondation Le Corbusier, Paris.

43. A. Mostakov, "Bezobraznoe nasledstvo arkhitektora E. Maia," *Arkhitektura SSSR*, 1937, no. 9:62.

44. Some sources claim that 571 industrial plants were designed by Kahn and his firm.

45. Philip A. Adler, "Stalingrad as I Saw It," *Detroit News*, 28 September 1942.

46. The Fagus Factory, one of the early projects designed by Walter Gropius in Germany, was considered one of the "ancestors" of modern industrial architecture.

47. Albert Kahn, "Architectural Trend," *Journal of the Maryland Academy of Sciences*, April 1931, no. 2.

48. Albert Kahn, *Pencil Points*, May 1932, 299.

49. The first exhibition of modern architecture, devoted in large part to European architecture, opened at the Museum of Modern Art of New York in 1932.

50. A partial list of Albert Kahn's projects in the Soviet Union is given in *Industrial and Commercial Buildings* (Detroit, Mich.: A. Kahn, 1936).

51. Undated clipping, archives of A. Kahn, Inc., Detroit.

52. Undated clipping, archives of A. Kahn, Inc., Detroit.

53. *Detroit Free Press*, 16 July 1942.

54. Ibid.

55. Quoted by Grant Hilderbrand, *The Architecture of Albert Kahn* (Cambridge: MIT Press, 1974), 128.

56. Note by Louis Kahn, "We Can Do Business with the Russians," 7 January 1944.

57. Letter dated 5 March 1931, National Archives, Washington, D.C.

58. Letter dated 22 April 1931, National Archives, Washington, D.C.

59. Letter dated 12 March 1931, National Archives, Washington, D.C.

60. Letter dated 13 July 1931, National Archives, Washington, D.C.

61. Letter dated 12 May 1931, National Archives, Washington, D.C.

62. *Detroit Free Press*, 4 March 1932.

63. *New York Times*, 25 March 1932.

64. In fact, Kahn depended heavily on American industry; many of the plants erected by his firm were manufactured in the United States then shipped to the USSR and assembled there. Machine tools and technical equipment were also imported from the United States.

65. Archives of A. Kahn, Inc., Detroit.

66. This and subsequent quotes come from Isadore Rosenfield's article

A. KOPP   published in *Soviet Russia Today,* a serial publication issued by the Soviet embassy in Ottawa, Canada.

67. No such list exists prior to 1933, when diplomatic relations between the United States and the Soviet Union were reestablished.

68. Dolores Hayden, *Seven American Utopias: The Architecture of Communitarian Socialism, 1790–1975* (Cambridge: MIT Press, 1975).

69. Nikolai Chernyshevskii, *What Is to Be Done?,* trans. Nathan Haskell Dole (New York: T. Y. Crowell, 1886).

70. The delegation consisted of five French architects, including the author.

ABOUT THE AUTHORS

MILKA BLIZNAKOV is Professor of Architecture and Urban Design at Virginia Polytechnic Institute and State University (VPI). A practicing architect, she has published extensively on the history of Soviet architecture, with particular emphasis on the Russian avant-garde. She founded a Resource Center for Studies of Women in Architecture at the College of Architecture and Urban Studies, VPI.

WILLIAM C. BRUMFIELD is Associate Professor of Slavic Languages at Tulane University. He is the author of *Gold in Azure: One Thousand Years of Russian Architecture* (1983), as well as articles on Russian literature and architecture. His work as a photographer of Russian architecture is in the permanent collection of the Photographic Archives of the National Gallery of Art, Washington, D.C.

ANATOLE KOPP is Professor of Planning at the University of Paris, VIII. Until 1983 he also worked as an architect on public projects for the French and Algerian governments. He has published widely in French and English, including books on Soviet architecture such as *Town and Revolution: Soviet Architecture and Planning of the Twenties* (1970) and *Constructivist Architecture in the USSR* (1985).

BLAIR A. RUBLE is Director of the Kennan Institute of Advanced Russian Studies at the Woodrow Wilson International Center for Scholars, Washington, D.C. He has published on a broad range of subjects in the Soviet field, with particular emphasis on social and political topics. His most recent book is *Leningrad: Shaping a Soviet City* (1990).

INDEX

Birth and death dates for Russian and Soviet architects are given in parentheses.